"In my humble opinion, this is the best book SARK has yet written. She brings her bright, colorful, upbeat energy to a very heavy subject. And helps us all lighten up and smile!"

CHristiane Northrup M.D.

author of *The Wisdom of Menopause* and *Women's Bodies, Women's Wisdom*

"In her unique and marvelous way, SARK shares her own story with humor and honesty, inspiring us with her wisdom. In *Glad No Matter What*, she shows us how to live with greater genuine happiness even when we're facing tough challenges or tumultuous change. I loved this book!"

MArci SHiMoff

New York Times bestselling author of *Happy for No Reason*

"SARK is one of the truly authentic voices in the world of personal transformation. There are no theories here. This book will take you on a journey straight to the heart, holding your hand every step of the way, and you will know you can relax completely in the care of a compassionate and wise guide. The whole world ought to read this book."

CHeri HuBer

Zen teacher, writer, and speaker and author of *There Is Nothing Wrong with You*

"Are you in the tender time between no longer and not yet? No need to freak out. SARK comes to the rescue with a wise, healing, and practical book that will help you find your way through loss and change. This book is like a wise girlfriend, a life coach, and a guru all rolled into one."

Joan Borysenko PH.D

psychologist and soul friend, author of
It's Not the End of the World: Developing Resilience in Times of Change

"It's easy to get caught up in one side of loss and change — adversity — especially in times like these. But there's another side of the coin — opportunity — that is so much bigger, fresher, and more abundant in the long run. In a masterful way that's almost a left brain/right brain tango, SARK has laid out the path for us to transform our lives no matter what the world throws at us."

CHip Conley

founder of Joie de Vivre hotels and author of *Peak*

THis is **NOT** A BOOK ABOUT feeling GLAD wHen you don't.
How annoying

THis **is** A BOOK ABOUT finding and LiviNg From THe GLAD pArts in **All** of your Feelings.

I CAll it prActiCAL GLADness

We can Be sAD/GlAD/MAd and More All AT once. MosT of us were not tAUGHT How To HOLD or NAVIGATe MULTiple Feelings. I've Been stuDyiNg and PrActiciNg Feelings Since I WAs tolD By My pAreNts To "Go to My room" and HAve My Feelings—and come out wHen I WAs "Feeling Better."

In My Approximately 50 YeArs of prActiciNg wiTH My Feelings, I've leArned THAT Feelings don't ever leAve us. We keep HAviNg THem and THis is Good!

THis BOOK will sHow you new wAys To experience and PrActice wiTH your FeeliNgs. THis Kind of "**PrActiCAL GlAdness**" will expAnd your cApAcities for **JOY** no MAtter wHAts HAppeNing.

THis BOOK will Also **support you** in occupying your SADness and oTHer Feelings in

NEW WAYS

THAT will sHorten THe lengTH of Time you need to experience THem. **YOU will still Feel** THe CHAllengiNg Feelings; YOU will JusT Be invited NOT TO spend so MucH Time and energy THere.

You can Feel GLAD More often

4

More Good Words for *Glad No Matter What*

"SARK has done it again. She's taken the harrowing life challenges of dealing with loss and change, turned them upside down, and created a powerful healing path that will calm fears, warm hearts, and transform lives forever. Way to go, SARK!"

CHeryL riCHArdson

author of *Take Time for Your Life* and *The Art of Extreme Self-Care*

"SARK lives her words — that's the most important thing — and her authenticity lends authority and power, and beauty and joy, to her writing. Whether you read through or dip into this book, you'll find helpful, life-affirming reminders on any page — not about positive thinking but about positive living."

D a n M i l l M a n

author of *Way of the Peaceful Warrior* and *The Four Purposes of Life*

"In *Glad No Matter What*, SARK reminds us that life presents each one of us with unique and incredible gifts all wrapped up in different ways. We each must delve deep down and find the courage to open those gifts and rejoice to see how they will change our soul. This book is your guide on how to open those gifts!"

J AMes Van PrAAGH

spiritual medium and author of *Unfinished Business*

"SARK has birthed yet another profound gift in her latest work, *Glad No Matter What*. She shows the gifts in healing from loss with her approachable and simple language, illustrating the kind of transformation that is possible as we dare to mend our broken hearts."

Kristine CArlson

author of *Heartbroken Open* and *Don't Sweat the Small Stuff for Women*

"SARK's wisdom, compassion, joy, and humor are among the brightest lights I know. In *Glad No Matter What*, she offers outstanding tools and inspiration to make everything you encounter work in your favor. I wish everyone would read this book and bring these heartful lessons to life!"

A L a n COHen

author of *A Daily Dose of Sanity*

"SARK gives you practical, real ways to find your joy. Happiness is in your ability to navigate the real-life ups and downs in a way that is honest and generates more 'gladness' and gratitude by being truthful about where you are. This is a wonderful and tangible book that will help so many authentically smile from the inside."

MAriel HeMingWAY
author, actress, health enthusiast, and adventurer

"*Glad No Matter What* is a powerful and honest companion on the journey to emotional healing. The book resonates with compassion and wisdom. Each page seems to say, 'You can trust me. I have been there. I will guide you.'"

Frederic Luskin PH.D
author of *Forgive for Good*

"*Glad No Matter What* is a profound and important book. SARK's passion, vulnerability, and wisdom are on display, as always! With this book, she shows us how to see the gift in difficulty and to transform loss in beautiful ways."

Mike Robbins
author of *Be Yourself, Everyone Else Is Already Taken*

"This reassuring, heart-lived book will be like a big poofy quilt wrapped around every reader, offering immense permission and kindness to truly be glad no matter what."

Jennifer Louden
author of *The Woman's Comfort Book* and *The Life Organizer*

"In *Glad No Matter What*, SARK shares the magic of multidimensional feelings. While reading this delightful, insightful book, I sobbed and laughed — often at the same time! (I didn't know this was possible, but I now highly recommend it.) If you have ever loved, lost love, or been crushed by grief…quick — grab this book and tightly hold on. It's a magnificent life preserver."

Arielle Ford
author of *The Soulmate Secret*

FEELING GLAD More often and more consistently is AVAILABLE for everyone in any circumstance.

IT DOES require practice and perspective shifting WHen we live AS A "splendidly imperfect" still-Growing HUMan Bean THere will Be an animated QUALITY To our lives.

THis animated QUALITY contains willingness, Flexibility, TruTH-telling, and deeper CAPACities for Love and JOY.

I AM A Life experimenter, A Deep emotional diver, and somewHAT of A psychological pioneer. I'M Also A Self-loving SOUL WHo is inconsistently BrAve and riddled wiTH Fears, DoUBTs and oTHer FLAWS too numerous to list Here.

I've Lived THrovGH A MArvelous CATALOG of Life experiences, which led me to want to SpeAK deeply ABouT THese topics and create THis BOOK.

I AM Also A loving, Growing HUMan Bean WHo is Avidly practicing Transforming WHAT Hurts into WHAT HeLps and inviting you To JOin me.

Beans love To Be Together

OTHER BOOKS BY SARK

GLAD NO MATTER WHAT

Transforming Loss and Change Into Gift and Opportunity

BY SARK

NEW WORLD LIBRARY

@ incandescent Thank you's to:

JASON, Kristen, MArc, Munro, Kim, Jonathan, Tona, Georgia, The whole **New World Library** Team

☀ any copy editing mistakes all mine

Photographs by SARK

New World Library 14 PAMAron WAY Novato CA 94949

© SARK 2010

Library of congress cataloging-in-publication available upon request

First printing, November 2010 ISBN 978-1-57731-935-1

☀ The LABYrinth on The cover is at Lands End in san francisco
☀ And yes we flipped The Golden Gate Bridge and The Marin Headlands on The back cover

New World Library is a proud member of The **Green Press** initiative

10 9 8 7 6 5 4 3 2

TABLE of Contents

11

7. portraits of JOY and Transformation Through change and loss

8. Acknowledgments, After note, TrausformAtion change sHeet

Feelings Menu for This Book

*CHOOSE HOW YOU FEEL RIGHT NOW, GO TO THAT SECTION

I FEEL:

- SCARED . . . . . . GO TO: SINGING THROUGH THE STORMS. page 92
- needing love . . . . GO TO: WAVES OF LOVE . . . . . . PAGE 43
- LOST . . . . . GO TO: YES TO ALL THE CHANGES . . . PAGE 72
- HAPPY . . . . . GO TO: Portraits of JOY and Transformation PAGE 205
- anxious . . . . . Go TO: SINGING THROUGH THE STORMS PAGE 92
- worried . . . . Go TO: SINGING THROUGH THE STORMS. PAGE 92
- SATISFIED . . . . Go TO: Glad NO Matter WHAT . . . . . PAGE 25
- excited . . . . . Go TO: Transformation Practices. PAGE 164
- Fearfull . . . . Go TO: SINGING THROUGH THE STORMS. PAGE 92
- angry . . . . . Go to: Transformation Practices. PAGE 164
- Hopeless . . . . Go to: WAves of Love . . . . PAGE 43
- curious . . . . . Go to: Portraits of Joy + Transformation PAGE 205
- resistant . . . . Go to: Transformation Practices. PAGE 164
- Joy·full . . . . Go to: Portraits of Joy + Transformation PAGE 205
- LOVING . . . . Go to: WAVES of LOVE. . . . . PAGE 43
- FLAT . . . . . Go to: WAVES of Love . . . . . PAGE 43
- inspired . . . . . Go to: Transformation Practices PAGE 164
- energized . . . . Go to: Yes to All The Changes PAGE 72
- Grieving . . . . Go to: Learning to see in The DARK PAGE 117

14

GLAD Introduction

I've learned about loss as we all do—by living it. I think of it as "learning by loss light."

I've also learned to find THE GIFTS within the losses—which is where THE GLAD part comes in. After my dad died, I experienced the death of my mother—whom I called "Marvelous Marjorie"—after helping to care for her in the last 3 years of her life. The following year, my beloved seventeen-year-old cat, Jupiter, died in my arms.

WHile writing this book, a significant love relationship changed shape and ended.

I Alchemized and transformed these significant losses into gifts that continue to nourish me today. Of course, I had to travel through these losses and feel and experience them deeply before beginning and continuing my

Transformative Journey

I've learned that trying to "skip to" the gladness doesn't work. The losses and grief will wait and insist upon being acknowledged. I remember just hoping that "bad things" wouldn't happen to me so I wouldn't have to feel bad.

This young emotional wish still pops up sometimes.

now i know how to take care of that part

Then I realized that bad things had already happened to me and I could choose how to respond.

Our transformative work is shown to us by the very difficulties and losses that happen to us

After the shock and time passing and lots of tears, I began doing my transformative work about my mother's death. For a very long while I felt guilty, angry, sad, and helpless because I couldn't save her or stop her from feeling pain or dying.

When I finally began accepting her death, I started my journey to find the gifts in it.

I call these "Gifts of Death," which spells GOD

I recalled all the incredible souls who had helped us in the three-year dying process. I then magnified my joy-full memories with my mom in her last years.

There were so many experiences that I filled pages and pages with written descriptions of my gratitude and gladness.

I also spent time learning and practicing how to forgive the grudges or guilt or anything else holding me back from purely loving my mom. Her death and life showed me how much we all

Affect each other

I FELT AMAZED THAT I WAS ABLE TO HELP provide care for Her, even After All of our difficulties. SHe WAS not an easy personality To deal wiTH!

and neither was I

I've learned THAT THere Are angels in HuMan forM and THAT "less THan angelic" people Are our perfect TeACHers for practicing COMPASSion and Acceptance.

My MoTHer's spirit continues To reveal GiFTS. Her dying process sHowed me How Absolutely fierce and strong I can Be. I Accessed rAGe and protectiveness THAT I'd HAD no ideA were wiTHin me, AS I nAViGATed THe HeALTH-care system and nursing Homes. I BecAMe THe "MoTHer GrizzLy BeAr" on Her BeHALF THAT I'd sometimes experienced Her As.

NOW I Know and feel THAT sHe's GlAd to Be deAd, and I'm GlAd THAT sHe Lived!

Her spirit communicATes Her GlAdness To me

When My CAT, Jupiter, died AFter 17 yeArs, I HeLD His soFT, no-longer-BreATHinG BODy in My ArMs and soBBed so HArd I could BArely BreATHe.

I truly didn't Know How I would Be Able to Live wiTHout THe unconditional love and pHysical presence of My MAGnificent CAT. AFter A long GrieVinG TiMe, I emerGed reAdy to experience THe GiFTS in THis deep loss.

17

Jupiter's Life and death filled me with fresh compassion for others—because I now knew how much loss could **seem** to take away. I looked at everyone with heartbreaking eyes of love, knowing that they had all walked or crawled through these kinds of losses too.

I experienced brand-new trust in the necessity of loving and of losing.

Of course, I wish **Jupiter** could have lived forever, but his necessary physical departure strengthened me in ways I couldn't have predicted. **Jupiter** helped me to trust death and love life even more deeply. His love imprinted me with indelible certainty that **unconditional love** was within me all along. Jupiter just showed me how to be able to see and experience it.

I feel that Jupiter's presence in my life and physical departure have infused me with grace and light.

I am now so glad
to share
that grace and light with the
W O R L D

My love relationship changing and ending is still pretty fresh, and I'm still grieving and finding the GIFTS. The main one right now is that we DARed To love each other despite significant distance, Age and Lifestyle differences.

I've learned THAT THE GIFTs of loss don't Always show up Quickly in The MATERial world. It can take MONTHS or YEARS of HEALING and Grieving Before THE GIFTs Are revealed.

I've seen and experienced over and over THAT Grief and loss Are A L W A Y S

D O O r WAys To Transformation

My experiences WITH BOTH HAVE SHowed me THAT We can MoVE Actively work W I T H TIME AS we process Grief and loss, instead of JUST WAITING For TIME to pAss. We really can consciously practice integrATING loss and Grief and Living WITH THem more fully and BeAutifully.

I KNOW NOW THAT THIS HEALING HAppens in SpirALs and LAyers and NOT in STEps Like A L A D D e r

We cycle BACK Around and stArt over, GeT stuck in THE Middle, and SOMETIMES GET TO WHAT Feels Like THE end 19

Quickly.

We can weave all of these experiences together into an eventually elegant tapestry. I've been speaking with lots of people about the subjects of loss and grief, and it's clear that in every case, whatever has been lost— job, savings, home, health, money life— has tremendous gifts and opportunities to offer

IF

we do our transformational work.

All the people I've been speaking with about loss are traveling through their own "loss layers." Most start out expressing feelings of anger or resistance and eventually seek out new experiences.

I spoke with a man who shared with me that he felt afraid that people loved him just for his wealth. Shortly after that, he lost a significant amount of money and all his property. He was newly engaged and begun to feel loved for the first time, and not for his money.

My friend and mentor Patricia experienced a major stroke at age 62 and needed to give up her home, career and pets. She speaks of feeling free and unencumbered, as well as sad and lost, and is now living with one of her daughters and family,

Doing deep Meditative work and JUST LiViNG Life.

I've witnessed so Many stories of losses Transformed into Gifts, and we All HAVe eXAMples of This Happening. MOST of us Know someone WHo HAs experienced, or HAVe ourselves experienced, A JOB loss, and THen lATer Transformed it into someTHing MUcH More rewardinG.

I HAD A wonder.full Mentor in THis reALM. Her NAMe WAs ISABeL, and Before sHe died AT AGe 90, sHe toLD me:

"WiTHOUT exception,
every loss or cHanGe in My Life HAs
AlwAys resvLTed in someTHing Good or Better!"

I Know THAT we can support ourselves and oTHers in creATively MAKinG THese perspective SHifTs and doing THis TransformAtive work of

C H a n G i n G

(H O W)

w e   r e s p o n D

T O   W H A T

HAppens T o   U S

THIS BOOK will show you NEW WAYS to practice.
We will benefit GREATLY From practicing
and experimenting with even EASIER WAYS TO

SHIFT
and
Trans. forM

MOST of us were Conditioned To Accept
and Live WITH "BAd News" and don't reALize
THAT it's

JUST
News

We can respond and not reACT and CHange
Our emotional CLIMATE.

HAVing permission, support, reminders
and eXAmples of Trans.forming losses and
CHanges into The GIFTS and Opportunities
THAT They Are is WHAT

THIS BOOK is ABOUT.

22

"THe secret of CHANGe is To
Focus All your energy Not on
FiGHTiNG THe OLD BuT on BuilDiNG
THe New"   SOCRATeS

screen   of contemplation

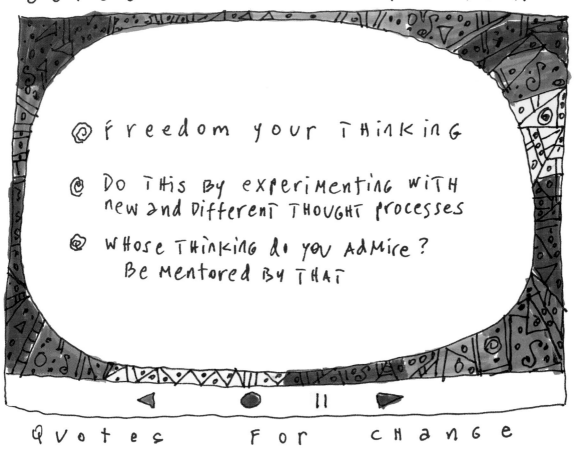

@ Freedom your THiNKiNG

@ Do THis By experimenting WiTH
new and Different THOUGHT Processes

@ WHose THiNKiNG do you AdMire ?
Be Mentored By THAT

Quotes   For   CHANGe

I
WiSH
You
JOY
WiTH
All My HeART
Jane Austen

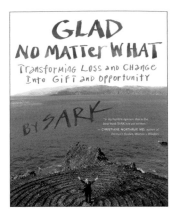

GLAD
NO MATTER WHAT
Transforming Loss and Change
Into Gift and opportunity

BY SARK

"Intention Bends
Towards The Light"
Joseph Campbell

BOOKS

- ◎ The Happiness project Gretchen Rubin
- ◎ instant CALM PAUL Wilson
- ◎ The end of fear Richard Schaub Ph.D
  with Bonney Gulino Schaub r.N.
- @ Start where you Are Pema Chödrön
- @ eat Mangoes Naked SARK
- @ The Art of emotional Healing Lucia
  Capacchione Ph.D
- @ energy Medicine Donna eden

Web resources

- ◎ forthelittleonesinside.com
- ◎ Goddessguidebook.com
- @ innertransformer.com
- @ ToriHartman.com
- ◎ DanMillman.com
- @ Livingcompassion.org
- @ drjudithorloff.com

Music

- ◎ Murielsings.com

☆ OTHer kinds of resources
- @ put 1/2 Box of Baking Soda
  in your BATH water. it Makes
  The water Alkaline which
  Promotes Good HEALTH
- @ Call My Inspiration phone line
  415.546.3742

"Believe THAT Life is Worth Living
and your Belief will create THAT FACT.
Be Not Afraid To Live"
William James

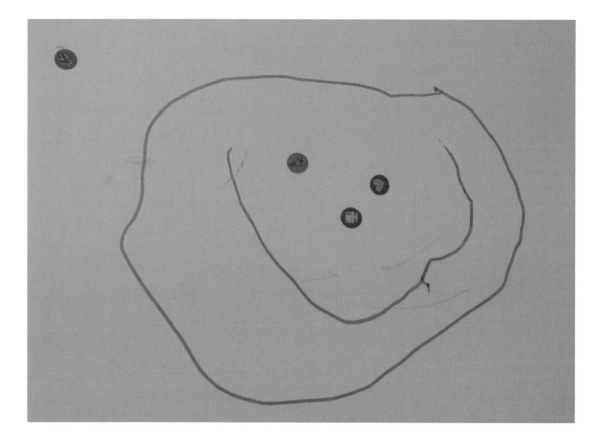

GLAD

No

MATTeR

WHAT

NOT GLAD AT ALL

It is As important To occupy THe "not GlAd" plAces As it is To Be GlAd.

Society Puts A lot of Positive Attention on Feeling GOOD, GlAd, WHole, HAppy, Confirmed, centered, Joy·full, exvberant, and THrilled. THese Are All GreAT Feelings, and As we know, THey dont and cannot lAsT.

We will All experience THe HiGHs and Lows and THe rich, fertile Middle sPAces of our Feelings on A continvous BAsis. LeArning To NAviGATe All THe spAces skillfully and ARTFully will Give vs STrong TOOLS To reAch For in All kinds of Times. If we dont prActice WiTH THose tools in Advance, we wont know HOw or WHAT To reAch For WHen we need THem.

Allowing yourself To Feel "not GlAd" WHen you do will ActuAlly Allow you to Feel GlAd More often.

IT works like THis:

"I Feel "not GlAd" But I will Hide it, Repress it, substitute oTHer THings, Deny it, lie ABout it, Avoid it, MAke up sTories To cover it up."

So "Not GlAd" is NoT Seen or HeArd and HAs NO CHOice BuT TO GeT LouDer

And "louder" looks like: unhappier, lost, hopeless, low hum of sadness, crabby, off center, negative self-talk.

Even 1-5 seconds of acknowledging a NOT GLAD feeling will cause this energy to be able to shift and change.
It looks like this:

"Not as bad as I thought, learning to accept what is, discovering new FACTS, asking for support, feeling a bit better than I did."

MOST of us avoid even the 1-5 seconds
WHY?

Because it feels familiar to be in pain and struggle.

We are more accustomed to these feelings and know all kinds of strategies and coping mechanisms: overeating or drinking, smoking, compulsive exercise or work, or just denying, avoiding lying or hiding.

These all **work** in the short term and **we know** it.

We don't know as much about the longer term or middle way, and it might feel mysterious or uncertain. Our skills here are just under- or undeveloped.

We all just want to "feel better," and this is good!

But HABITUALLY trying to avoid feeling bad leads us to feeling worse. Losses multiply, grief stacks up, and then we often "strike ourselves down" with illness, depression or other setbacks that we then blame on outside circumstances.

Go to the feelings menu in the front of this book, look up how you feel in this moment, and read from the sections indicated. You can just do this randomly. Remember that you might be feeling a combination of feelings. Of course, our feelings shift and change frequently—sometimes literally in the time it takes to blink your eye.

We don't trust this, and think if we identify or name a feeling, it could or will grow and crush some part of us to death.

Actually, the opposite occurs—if we can acknowledge our feelings, they can then transform. Sometimes feelings feel so excruciating, it seems clear that we cannot live with or through them.

If you closely follow a child, or the child parts in yourself and observe them feeling their feelings, you will notice a flow of feelings one to another—like movements of water.

FEELINGS ARE in MOTION THIS WAY, not stuck and OBSESSED over LikE ADULTS' FeeliNGS sometimes ARe. I LiKE TO CAll it "THe rACCooN FeAtvre" WHEN WE GO over and over A FeeliNG, HOLDiNG it in our little pAws LikE A rACCooN, and we don't or can't put it down.

And THen THere's no room THere For A new FeeLiNG To A r i s e.

In order To promote THe Flow of FeeliNGS...

START noticiNG and speAkinG of your FeeliNGS differently. See if you can consciovsly experiment WiTH MVLtiple FeeliNGS. For exAMple, iMAGine A Good Friend cHANGiNG A plan and your response BEiNG: "of course I understand! I Feel A Bit disAppointed THAT I won't see you, BUT I Also Feel GlAd To HAve some extrA Time for Myself."

THis WAY, you're HonoriNG BOTH FeeliNGS siMultaneously. So often, we don't AcknowledGe THe DisAppointed feeliNG or THe GlAd FeeliNG. WHEN we can experience and express MVLtiple feeliNGs, we Are expanding our eMotionAL CApAcities.

IF you don't Feel reAdy To sHAre your FeeliNGs out loud, you can write THem down and experiment WiTH nvances or little Bits of FeeliNGs and NAMe THem As soon As you can identify THem. THis will Give you an expanded FeeliNGs lanGvAGe To work WiTH.

As you experience the flow of feelings more often, you will begin to trust your feelings and make more space for them.

This will create a way for feelings to move and change more frequently.

As your feelings change, you will be in motion yourself, able to move gracefully from anger or despair to sadness to hope.

It's like an emotional dance party: Some dances will be your favorites — others more awkward or difficult to learn. Some will be boring or make you mad. Some you will wish you never needed to do again. But AHA! you think. I will dance all the dances I can.

FEELING GLAD WHEN YOU DO

One of the great things about doing these Transformative practices is the capacity for more gladness more of the time. Sometimes people get so occupied by other kinds of feelings, that they really don't experience gladness very often at all.

I created a daily—or sometimes—practice to help myself navigate through CHALLENGING feelings and allow the gladness too. It's called:

Three Part Harmony

You'll want to have a pen and paper, or if you write more easily on a computer, use THAT. It will take between 5-30 minutes, and **5 minutes** is a good starting point.

PART 1 of the HARMONY is

M A D P A G E S

@ Across the top of a piece of*paper write any and all words to describe CHALLENGING feelings you may be having right now: **worried,** scared, frustrated, furious, overwhelmed, anxious, angry, intolerant, annoyed, irritated, confused MAD, and so on.

*i use recycled paper or backs of paper for these

⊚ THEN, MAKE A **FAST List** of everything you can think of THAT's causing you to feel the feelings you listed, small to large. LET yourself get very dramatic and THEATRICAL. Use lots of exclamation points.
They love to be overused

underline THings, abbreviate. Don't think about it. just write. GET it All out. Write until you can't think of one more thing. It sometimes takes me 6-8 pages. sometimes less You're not going to share these pages with anyone, so don't censor yourself.

⊚ WHen you've finished, TAKE 3 deep breaths. FOLD THE PAGES and Address THEM TO THE universe, or GOD, or whoever you think is larger THan you.

⊚ This Action is often enough to begin transforming These kinds of THOUGHTS. It "clears THE WAY," and when THEY return, THEY won't HAVE THE SAME impact or **velocity**— Because A process HAS occurred. You've let THEM "speak," and in THAT space From your HEAD TO THE pAGE, THEy can change SHApe. HuMor can enter; equilibrium can return.

equilibrium loves to return

PART 2 of THE HARMONY
is
W i s e   P A G E S

- **I** Like To write "Wise voice Gladly speAKs" Across THe top of A piece of pAper

- **Your wise self** is THe sAme As your HiGHer self, nurturing pArt, Good pAreut or HiGHer spirit. Its THe pArt THAT's WiTH you All THe Time: **reAssuring**, reminding supporting **encourAGing** — pure positive energy representing unconditionAl love.

- **TAKe out your MAd pAGes** and let your **wise self** respond To eAcH item you've written

Your wise self is very kind and knowing and sees you only WiTH Benevolent eyes. Write reAssuring, comforting and supportive comments.

use endeArMeuts

Let your wise self reAlly "speAK" to you THrouGH THe writing, and you will Be surprised AT All it HAs To offer. AT First, you MiGHT FeeL like you're MAKing THings up, and THAT's perfectly Fine. THe words will HAve A Good effect eiTHer WAY.

As you GAin experience and prActice tuning in To your **wise self,** you will HAve GreATer Access To THis pArt All THe Time, **even wHen you're not writing responses. THis will HAve A power·full effect on** your Feelings, Moods and responses to yourself and oTHer people.

I use endearments when writing as my wise self, like: Honey darling angel face, and I can feel it transforming my mood almost immediately.

After your wise self has responded and reframed everything on the mad pages, you can rip up and recycle those, because the thoughts and feelings have now shifted.

Save your wise voice pages to reflect on later.

i keep a special folder for my wise voice pages

wise
voice
gladly
speaks

PART 3 of THe HARMONY
is
GLAD PAGES

YOU COULD CAll THiS GRATE·FUll, GOOD THiNGS,
HAPPY TiMES, or JUST GLAD.
@ **Write Across THe TOP of A piece of pAPer**
All THe DeliciOUS eMOTiOns YOU CAN THiNk of: elATed,
JOY·FUll, THrilled, HAPPY, LUCKY, GreAT, overJOYed.
@ **MAKe A liST** of everyTHiNG YOU FEEL GLAD or
GrATeFUll For. I AlsO include THiNGS THAT Are in THe
ProcesS of TrAusForMiNG, SVCH As certAin kinds of
sADnesses THAT I'M GlAd AbOUT Feeling.*

* **remember** THAT YOU're PrActiciNG WeAVinG TOGeTHer
MVLTiple Feelings siMULTaueOUSLY

DOiNG PArts I and 2 of THe THree-pArt HARMONY
CleArs THe WAY for noticiNG and welcoMiNG More
GlADness. THiS THree-pArt HARMONY prActice sets YOU
UP For feeliNG GLADness More often, More purely,
and More cleArly. THen WHen oTHer kinds of FeeliNGs
Arise, YOU HAVE A WAY TO ALcHeMiZe and TransforM
THem.
InsteAd of sAyiNG "FeeL Better" TO yourself and
OTHers, sAY JVST one word:

FEEL

HELP THE WORLD BY BEING GLAD

G ive
L ovingly
A nd
D Aringly

People wonder All The Time, "How can I Help The worLD?"

One of The very BeST WAYS is To Be GIAd. GLAD People Give More, and Give More creAtively.

"Don't Ask yourself WHAT The worLD needs. Ask yourself WHAT MAKES you come Alive and THen Go DO THAT. BeCAUSE WHAT THe worLD needs is People WHo HAve Come Alive"
Dr. HowArd THUrMAn

And As you know, THis Does NOT MeAn Being GIAd All The Time, BUT GIAd More often.

AFTer A INGe eNTHQUAKe HAppened in HAiti, A 7 yeAr OLD Boy in London spoke From His GIAd HeArT and sAid, "I want to HeLP in HAiti and rAise Money By riding My Bicycle." He HAd rAised $500 WHen A news sTAtion GIAdly picked UP The story.

A week later, He HAd rAised $250,000.

There Are literally countless Glad Heart Stories, and I recommend reading them, steeping yourself in Them and reminding yourself THAT THEy Are Always GOing On, and THAT you HAVE A GlAd HEART too.

We want To HEAR WHAT your GlAd HEArt SAYS

Your idea MIGHT FIRST APPEAR TO BE AS UNLIKELY AS An upside down elepHant and turn into SOMETHING JUST AS SUBSTANTIAL.

The Real Story of Pollyanna

All my life I've heard people say to me,
"Oh, you're just such a Pollyanna."
Pollyanna is thought of as some kind of
positive ninny who naively tried to disregard
"tough times."

The Truth is, Pollyanna is the fictional story
of a young girl whose parents had died, and she was
sent to live with relatives she didn't know, in a small town.
She invented "The Glad Game" and relentlessly
found something good in every situation, even though
she was living through her own tough times. By doing
this, she transformed the town.

Finding gifts and gladnesses in every situation
does not mean disregarding pain, sorrow or suffering.

It means that you choose to see the gift
in every situation, and believe it's always there.

And it's a joy to practice! If you choose to find and see "THE BAD," you will.

It really is THAT simple.

People practicing and sharing GLADNESS are GIFTS TO THE WORLD, no matter what circumstances are happening.

I choose to Live Life as a "real" **Pollyanna** and to share a life made of goodness and gladness.

i've been happily engaged in this all my life and it's
A Life Full of Miracles

I invite you to join me if you're not already practicing this.

Here's a badge from 1913 that you can cut out or copy, and wear.

"Dance till the stars
come down with the rafters;
Dance, Dance,
Dance till you 'drop"
W. H. Auden

screen of contemplation

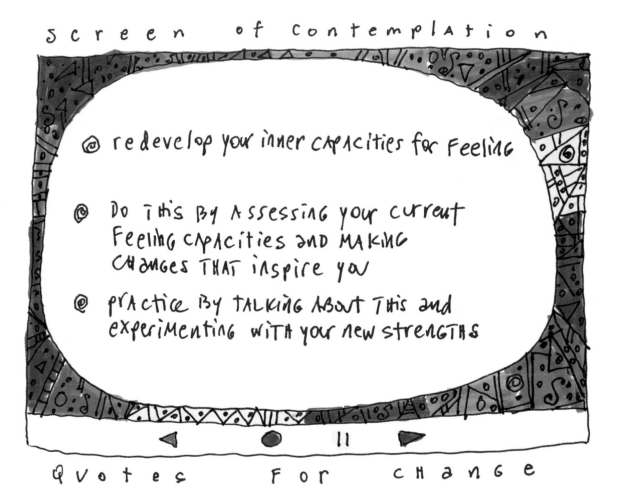

@ redevelop your inner capacities for feeling

@ Do this by assessing your current
feeling capacities and making
changes that inspire you

@ practice by talking about this and
experimenting with your new strengths

Quotes for change

"everything will be okay
in the end. If it's not
okay, it's not the end"
unknown author

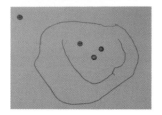

G L A D
N O
M A T T E R
W H A T

"TODAY I open my
HEART's Hand To
Allow The touch of Hope"
Julia Cameron

BOOKS

- Paranoia is The antidote
  For Paranoia rob Brezsny
- This Time I Dance! Tama Kieves
- Stumbling on Happiness Daniel Gilbert
- Broken open Elizabeth Lesser
- Pollyanna eleanor H. porter
- Happy For No reason Marci shimoff
- Be yourself, everyone else is Already Taken
  Mike robbins
- Living Juicy SARK
- Pass it on Joanna Macy

Web resources

- Good news network. org
- Happy For No reason. com
- innerlinks. com
- JenGray. com
- 1000Awesomethings. com
- Cherihuber. com
- vanessacarlisle. com

Music

- Karendrucker. com

☆ OTher kinds of resources
- Play The Transformation Game
  "A Game About The way you play your
  Life" innerlinks. com

"The Aim of Life is To Live,
And to Live means To Be Aware.
Joyously, drunkenly, serenely,
divinely Aware" Henry Miller

W A V e s

o f

L o v e

eXQuisite self-love and care
especially during times of loss and change

The subject of self love is often misunderstood. It's usually thought of as egotistical or self serving.

In its purest and most simple form, it is YOU loving YOU so that you can truly love others.

We Are All in long-term relationships with ourselves and have an opportunity to practice loving ourselves the way we wish others would love us.

We are not **taught** or guided about how to actually **feel** self-loving. We're just expected to be able to do it without **examples, teachers, role models** or permission to support ourselves as self-loving souls.

Certainly we're not supposed to talk about it!

If we hear someone say, "I'm so in love with myself," we might think that they're narcissistic or self-absorbed or selfish. We might even laugh nervously because it's so unusual.

If more people declare themselves to be self-loving, it will become marvelously common and everybody will begin doing it. When we talk about self-love, it can multiply and expand and **spread to others.**

Consider asking someone:

"How well are you loving yourself today?"

I asked my mail carrier how well He was loving Himself, and He smiled widely, put down the mail, and just stood there reflecting. After a few moments, with a little self-loving smile, He said:

"I am so glad you asked me that today! Now I'm going to go get myself a little gift after work."

I walked away smiling and feeling love from our exchange.

During a radio interview with 2 Hosts, I spontaneously asked How well they were loving themselves. One of the Hosts laughed and immediately responded:

"I'm loving myself so well! I'm just completing
a 30 day yoga challenge, and afterwards
I walk through a park and share love
with as many people as I can reach."

I felt uplifted and rather amazed by the answer, and kind of reluctantly asked the second Host the same question. He said: "I'm practicing loving All the parts of me. I'm doing mirror work right now and sending love to the parts of my body that I have previously ignored or even hated."

i felt amazed by His answer

45

Practicing self-love can be infinitely more challenging when we are immersed in sadness, loss, change, or if we are feeling frantic, out of control or scared of letting go.

Many of us will discontinue self-loving practices — if we ever had them — at that point. We might retreat into isolation, addictions, or other strategies to avoid or try to "wall off" loss or grief.

and no wall is lasting

Some part of us knows this doesn't work, but sometimes we can't help it.

Establishing a foundation of self-love practices in advance gives you tools to use during times of loss or change.

Practicing self-love will work also in the midst of loss or change. I will share a menu of self-love practices, and you can try the ones that resonate with you.

When you don't feel self-loving at all

The point is **NOT** to feel self-loving all the time. The point is to practice loving yourself as consistently as you are able, in all kinds of conditions. We tend to idealize new systems and think things like, "Loving myself—that sounds good, I shall do that." And the minute we fail, falter or lose our grip we judge that we're not being

self-loving enough

It's not true! It's all part of the practice. Isn't it odd that when we love others, we **know** that they'll disappoint or upset us along the way, but we don't give our very selves the same leeway?

What about when we experience self-hatred, self-neglect, despair, deep loneliness, or self-avoidance?

It really is simple.

Feel those too

I didn't say it was easy. Simple is not the same as easy. It can feel counterintuitive to deliberately feel what seems to be making you miserable, but the feelings will just keep clamoring and growing until you

Feel them

I've Been experimenting WITH self-HUGGING for A number of years now and HAVE Been HAVING profound experiences of FEELING Grounded and loving Myself THROUGH HUGGING, DURING All Kinds of emotions — especially turbulent ones.

For years, I understood These Things intellectually, But I didnt Know How To TAKE THAT understanding into My Body.

Here's one of THE THINGS THAT I do:

I curl up on My side and wrap My ARMS TiGHTly Around Myself and rock Gently BACK and forTH, while saying out loud:

"I'm right Here, I'm right Here, I'm right Here"

Over and over, until THe words lose Meaning.

THese words and sounds sooTHe some primitive PArts of Me THAT Are seeking love or reassurance.

I've learned THAT My BODY and soul HAVE needs THAT My Mind doesnt necessarily understand. you MIGHT WISH To creAte A customized version of THIS for yourself, or try Mine.

48

Sometimes I wish that loved ones would say certain things, in certain ways, and I've learned NOT TO WAIT or wish for others to do specific things but instead give myself WHAT I SAY I'M wanting.

So I send text messages to my own phone and then reread them whenever I need to.

Here's an example of one I recently sent to myself:

You are the sweetest DARLING FACE. I love you so much, dearest Susan. You're so BRAVE and GOOD to travel and share love and learning. enjoy every smidgen of GOODNESS and remember THAT I AM Always Here. You Are deeply, completely loved, and There is NOTHING MISSING. All is well. Allow your tears and The mysteries of loving other HUMANS. EACH tear MAKES room For more love, and it is All in divine order and TIMING. THere is no need To Look into The Future. Be Here now and Allow it All. I L o v e y o u

It's Also important To realize THAT if you're Feeling A strong emotion like self-HATred, it probably will not work To try To just jump to self-love.

You'll want To inch your WAY Along By Feeling someThing A Bit Better first

49

And Then continue inching

It's also a mistake to compare yourself in any way to someone else and the self-love or self-care or love from others that you imagine they're feeling and experiencing.

Everyone is practicing loving and caring for themselves and are all at different stages or places— different than you can possibly imagine.

Experiment with asking other people if they feel self-loving. Most likely very few people will express feeling self-loving in the moment that you ask.

People often project onto me that I must be incredibly self-loving because I talk about it, write books about it, teach classes, give interviews and write in bright colors yes.

I am truly in love with me

And, it's important to realize that I'm most often talking about

The practicing of self-love

and what has or hasn't worked for me or others.

I'm not always good at it!

Often while writing and creating art, I'm able to access a kind of spiritual channel—this channel contains wisdom beyond my human understanding.

50

I Listen closely and carefully, and write down
WHAT it SAYS, and SHARe THe MeSSAGeS in My BOOKS.

Sometimes its just Human me, stumbling Along...

WHen I CATCH Myself idealizing anyone—including
Myself— I do My Transformational WeAViNG practices
and put Myself

BACK in THe Middle

WHere Most self-loving TAkes place.

If and WHen you don't FeeL self-loving,
consider it AS A

GrADuATion of AwAreness

and reALize THAT you're ActiveLy leArning To
Love yourself

unconditionally
PrActice loving yourself in All of your
diMensions, not just WHen you ACT or lOOK
"Good."

and especially when you don't

WAYS TO exquisitely care for your self

How well and exquisitely do you care for your self?
WHAT does it look Like and Feel Like to do so?
CARING For ourselves in mind, BODY, emotions and spirit
can be overwhelming if we try to do it **perfectly** or All
AT once.

Sometimes when I read "tips" for self-care, especially
in popular magazines, I wonder why they don't make more
reference to people's "ACTUAL LIVES." These DAYS some
MAGAZines do, which is A wonderful reflection of more
people exquisitely caring for THEMselves!

Our ACTUAL Lives can be really Messy, inconsistent,
and filled with unexpected HUMAN THINGS: illness, needs of
love relationships, Broken technology, surprising requests,
Shocking news, people moving or ASKING FAVors...

I'M ALWAYs AMUsed By what pops up in My Life
When I'm creating A BOOK. This Time, My BROTHER Got
MARried, with me officiating, My Building partners requested
That we paint The outside of The Building, My love relationship
ended, A neighbor next door suddenly gutted Their 4 story
Building and started using JACKHAMMers and NAIL Guns From
8–5 each Day. And, if This All WASn't enough, The very
subject of The personal losses and changes I WAS writing About
were causing **debilitating Grief episodes.**

GOOD THING I WAS writing A BOOK About
Being GLAD No Matter WHAT!

THEN I GOT SICK.

My new PUBLISHER GRACIOUSLY GAVE me an extension of Time, WHICH I've now decided is

ex · Tension

I didn't plan for All THese FActors.

Self-cAre opportunities present THemselves DAily, and I expanded my practices of self-love in The Midst of These cHanges and CONDitions. I ASKed For more and different kinds of support, provided myself with extra cAre and kindness, and continued my daily self-cAre rituals and routines.

i Also stumbled, FAiled and ForGOT
To ASK For support

We All HAVe AreAs of self-cAre THAT will Benefit From cHange or expansion, AreAs THAT we HAndle well, or Better THAn other ones, and AreAs THAT we Deny or Hide From.

All THe wHile, opportunities for self-cAre continue. Many people cAre for others in Addition To cAring For THemselves: CHildren, elders, AnimAls, Businesses.

All of THese will Benefit even more By your exquisitely cAring for your self.

first and All WAYS

It doesn't need to be expensive or inconvenient for you to care for yourself exquisitely, and the more you practice, the better it becomes.

It's a "retuning" of your awareness and a fresh perspective about the value of self-care and your worthiness in being cared for.

Lots of people think they don't deserve self-care. They're afraid to take up space or time, or even admit to having needs.

We all have needs

we all have needs

we all have needs

you get the point

Some people provide care for themselves more naturally and organically than others do, and I'm suggesting that they mentor others in this.

One of the most important qualities for self-care is

primary permission

If you can't or haven't yet given yourself primary permission for self-care, consider this as a sign for you to begin, or to resume what you may have practiced earlier.

54

When we give ourselves primary permission, all sorts of things can happen:

1. We put ourselves first
   and find out that other people are usually happy for us—not like we may have feared. And for the times they wish we'd put them first, we can explain how we are blessing ourselves with exquisite self-care and invite them to join us or ask them for support.

2. We engage in life differently
   and act more eccentrically, asking people for uncommon things: extra candles, blankets, flowers, chocolate, kindness, reassurance, surprises. We may begin to talk with other people more deeply about our discoveries.

3. We make a commitment to self-care — the exquisite kind
   We consider what we need in the moment, remembering that the mind alone is an unreliable guide. We must engage body and emotions also. This commitment is an imperfect and continuing practice.

We commit to learning to ask for and receive support

When we are caring for ourselves, we discover that there is actually plenty of time and energy to care for others and the world too. It is not negatively "selfish" to care for yourself brilliantly and exquisitely. In fact, as you fill your own well from the inside and tend to your self with great love, it will naturally and effortlessly "spill over" for others to appreciate and utilize.

When you see someone who radiantly glows from within, you are seeing a self-caring soul. This kind of self-care is a living example to be inspired by, so that you can live that way also.

When you are exquisitely caring for yourself, you might feel flexible, kind, amused, curious, eager, enthusiastic or blessed. And for the times you don't feel things like this — in the inevitable times of fear, loss, anxiety or anger — self-care will support you even more.

I walk around in this world asking people for all sorts of things, and bestowing gifts and receiving gifts everywhere I go. I consider each of us to be a "Minister of Love."

When people are acting in less than loving ways, I think of the author and teacher Iyanla Vanzant, who reminds us: "He or she is a child of God, cleverly disguised as a ⸺⸺⸺."

56

It's All A Marvelous combination of Loving or Not loving

Recently I was Flying first class From new york To San Francisco and feeling very glad and gratefull for The extra leg room and Amenities.

Then we made an unscheduled stop and emergency landing to provide cure for A Man who had experienced A Heart Attack on The Flight.

We found out later THAT He HAD Lived

We Then SAT on The Ground on The plane for 5 Hours while They Got More required oxygen tanks So we could Take off Again. I looked Around + see WHAT I could offer. Helped The Flight Attendants Hand out drinks and snacks, and Then traded seats with various Passengers— A woman who was in pain from A recent Hip replacement, and A Mom and Her Baby. These people were glad to Be cared for in This way, and I Felt glad To offer.

Self-Caring people can Better provide care for others and practice receiving care too!

Self-care Also Multiplies. The More you practice, The More ways you'll find to exQuisitely care for yourself and for others.

WHEN I GO to A doctor, I cNe for Myself By ALTERING TheIr FORMS to reAd "client" or "person" insteAd of "pAtient."

since I'm rATHer impAtient, I really dont Feel Like A pAtient. Also, I find The word pAtient to imply some kind of Helplessness—ALTHOUGH I'm chAnGING THAT As my BODY AGes and chANGes

I Also chANGe where it sometimes says "Chief complAint" to reAd "celebrAtion of My HEALTH." DURING the Appointment, I BEGIN By Briefly celebrATING All THAT is working well In my BODY and ASKING The doctor or prActitioner to Join me in observing WHAT looks, or is, Good. If There Are HEALTH issues to resolve, I Ask for clear, positive lANGUAGE, and I ASK MYSELF For My Belief in My ABILITY to leArn and chANGe. I reQuest clear and simple Guidelines To Follow.

I've HAd doctors spontAneously HUG me, leAve Grinning, and MAKE chANGes To Their intAke forms. I've Also experienced Doctors who resisted me, defended Their policies and refused to Join me in any kind of celebrATION.

* In those cAses, I sAy to Myself:

"OH! It's A Doctor, cleverly disguised As A Jerk."

* THank you to Iyanla VanzAnt for shAring Her teAchings with The world

I will exquisitely care for myself consistently in any case and am glad to say that there are FAR MORE people who celebrate than there are those who refuse to.

During times of loss and change, it's incredibly important to draw from our well of self-love and care. THAT WAY, we stay centered and creatively expressive and are better able to offer our love and services to ourselves and the world.

Loss of Love

The perception that we have "lost love" is one of the most challenging losses and changes in our human experience that I can think of. Shortly before I began a first draft of this book, my love relationship of a year and a half changed, transformed, and ended. we were calling it a "**BREAKTHROUGH**" instead of a **BREAKUP**, which sounded evolved at the time — now in the actual living of it, I'm not so sure.

Perhaps better in theory than practice

I've also been experiencing breakdowns during this process.

One of my friends and mentors said to me:

"Don't make the mistake of attaching love to a person. remember that love flows from the source of all love, and is reflected by a person, but **is not in** that person."

It's very easy and tempting to think that it is in that person.

when my very dear younger brother, andrew, moved away, I wrote a poem about missing him:

60

The andrew shaped Hole

There is A Hole in my HEART
SHAped Like A BroTHer NAMed andrew
I'M sure if He cAlled, THe Hole would
Be filled
But THe Filling is FAlse
THe nexT Hole will Appear
NAMed someTHing else.
I'M discontinuing THe Hole-Filling
And focusing on wHo Feels THe Holes
in THe first place.

Now I'M practicing THis AGAin WiTH My
"lost" love. THe Grief experience is so unBelievABly
difficult to NAViGAte sometimes. HUGe wAves of 6rief
Arrive and I Feel certAin THAT I wont survive — But I do,
and THen wish I HAdn't, As anoTHer BiG wAve AppeArs.
THen on oTHer DAys, THe wAves Are so smAll or THe wAter
is FlAT and I'm sure THAT I'M "BeTTer" and THe Grief is "Gone."

Then a new memory floods in and the waves resume.

My words seem so ineffectual even describing this. Some of it feels so primitive and perhaps **pre-verbal.**

I've identified an aspect inside myself that knows only:

There

or

Not There

And if that aspect feels that "someone" or a certain feeling of love is **not** there, it can feel profoundly despairing.

Many people experience some version of this.

Some old coping mechanisms reappeared for me in the early stages of grief: emotional eating episodes, isolating and dwelling in sadness, hatred of romantic movies or songs and doing anything to avoid them.

Some new or healthier behaviors have also surfaced or continued:

Daily beach walks, new social adventures, increased ability to be vulnerable with others, crying more freely, and the sometimes **happily** obsessive cleaning and reorganizing of my living space— the revisioning of my physical surroundings can have a helpful effect on my grieving life. **Also, good therapy.**

sometimes I am just curled into a little ball sobbing

THIS "love loss" FeeLing is universAL and
so many Movies, songs and books Have Been created About
This subject.

I Am convinced THAT we All HAVe some form of
"love AMnesiA" BecAuse if we truly remembered How
Much it can Hurt, we would probably never try loving
AgAin. we Are convinced in our Amnesic STATe THAT
eACH TiMe and eACH new love relAtionship is

Different

especially in The Beginning, in WHATS called THe
"romance" or "HoneyMoon" pHAse or As my former TherApist
used to describe it:

"you Like To eAT dirt?
I like to eAT dirT too!"

THen we enter into WHATS sometimes called "THe
power struggle" or "individuATion" pHAse. It's wHere
we discover and experience THe Differences More
THan THe similArities.

it's Also WHere THe MAjority of couples "BreAk up"

If we can learn to nAvigAte THe Differences, we
MigHT choose to keep prActicing life and love with THAT
person, and if we're Lucky or committed enough To
TrAvel THrough THe first Two pHAses, we MigHT experience
THe pHAse called "MATure" or "committed" love. WHere
we Live in THe "Middle places" with another soul.

63

I'M currently practicing MATure love with myself. PErHAPS Life will Bring me A person to practice with or I will CHoose A new person; I'm not sure.

In The ending of A love relationship, THe worst PArt for me is THe letting go process — letting Go of THE language we spoke together, THe SHAred Microscopic memories, dreAMS, plans, and Knowing All THe DetAils About another person and also Being witnessed in My Life.

I'm so Glad to say in certAin wAys, I'd not felt More intimate with another HuMan Being THan I did In THis recently TransforMed love relationship — and THAT; of course why I wish it could HAve or would HAve continued.

we were Also Bi coastal THe whole time, with SigNificant Age and lifestyle Differences. THese FActors were eventually Just too lAr6e and numerous To Be workABle, and THE Truth was THAT we Finally reAlized THAT neither of us wanted to work on THem! So we saw A THerapist, cried, TALKed, tried, Fought, Confessed, SHared, and in the end, BOTH of us:

LeT   Go

It still Hurts sometimes THAT I can't "solve it," Fix it, or "MAKE it work." THe pART of me THAT still AttAcHes love To another person is sure THAT I'll die From THis pAin.

Luckily, I HAVE A wise Adult self who knows THAT THis too will CHange, FAde, and Become something else.

I Am Alchemizing it even As I write This

One of THe many GiFTs of losses is THAT THe More we consciously experience THem, THe More we intrinsically know we can transcend THem THe next Time.

And of course, its not an Accident THAT I'M writing A BOOK CAlled "GlAd No MATTer WHAT" AT THe same time THAT my love relationsHip is ending and cH anging. Because I Must eventually emerge From THe tears and rAge and Ambient sAdness and Grief To Find THe Gladnesses Here too, Mixed in with THe sadnesses.

I Feel so sAd:

- THAT we meT AT AGes 32 aud 55 aud found THe AGe Difference too CHallenGinG to nAviGATe
- THAT we Lived on opposite COASTS aud THAT it seemed impossible for eiTHer person To Move
- THAT "love wAsnt enouGH" aud BoTH of us would HAve needed to commit to siGnificant Life cHanGes for our relAtionsHip to Grow aud continue
- THAT I MeT someone to love wHo wAs aud is so exceptionAL, aud it couldnt continue in THe romantic form.

I AM so GlAd:

- THAT we meT eACH oTHer aud loved so Deeply.
- THAT our BreAKTHrouGH/BreAK up process wAs Mutually cHosen aud Haudled respectfuly.
- THAT we souGHT wise professionAL counsel aud invested our Time, Money, aud enerGy in THe process.

I AM Beyond GlAd to HAve loved aud Been loved so well, truly aud deeply, aud to HAve experienced such profound HeART openinG. We intend aud Hope To Kuow eACH oTHer in some form As our Lives continue. we recoGnized THAT we love eACH oTHer on A Deeper level THAT's More THan THe relAtionsHip form we were in, aud seT eACH oTHer free To

66

experience new love relationships.

If she has a child someday, I hope to be its "fairy godmother." Still, from this freshly grieving place, it's somewhat agonizing to write about and feel that because I thought there was a possibility we'd be life partners and held a tiny hope that perhaps I could be a parent too.

A long held dream of mine

I love to feel this grief because these tears are the language of the grieving parts, and my deep sadness is evidence of the remarkable heart openings and shared love I experienced.

I hate to feel this grief because it feels so messy, out of control, and just plain sad.

I am weaving a luminous nest in between love and hate, gladness and sadness. In this luminous nest are Acceptance, Allowing, realizations, wonder, and mystery.

it is the middle place

This rich, fertile middle is the place I most often live now. Now I know how to stay out of the living in extreme emotions, I feel a profound sense of peace.

I trust THE SADNESS and MY HEART'S CAPACITIES. I can sometimes welcome THE tears and put my Hands out for THE lessons. Sometimes I Hide in THE TV or OTHER Activities To **MASK THE PAIN.**

Sometimes I Feel Like MY BiG BrAin is so vividly stupid it is BREATHTAKING. I try To "THink" MY WAY out of pAin, and MY Feelings All WAit Like BABY chicks to Be Fed.

Sometimes I can turn to MY Feelings and tenderly HoLD THem, or CALl for support. every DAY I TAKE MY Feelings on WALks, and sometimes when we return, I lock THem in THe closeT. But MY Feelings Always return, HAving leArned long AGo **How To survive any storm.**

By THE Time you reAd THese words About MY trAnsformed love relAtionship, I will HAve CHAnGed siGnificantly in THis reALm

68

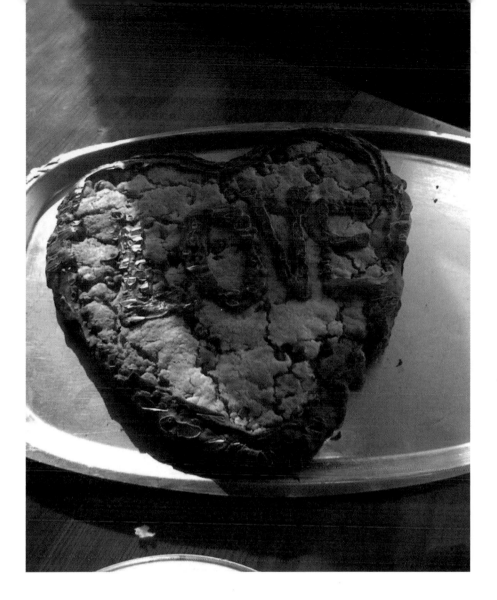

During the midst of our love affair, our friend
annie baked us this enormous cookie of love.
I like to think that we're both still enjoying it,
together or not.

"NOTHING is eiTHer Good
or BAd But THiNKiNG MAKes
it So"

SHAKespeAre

screen   of   contemplation

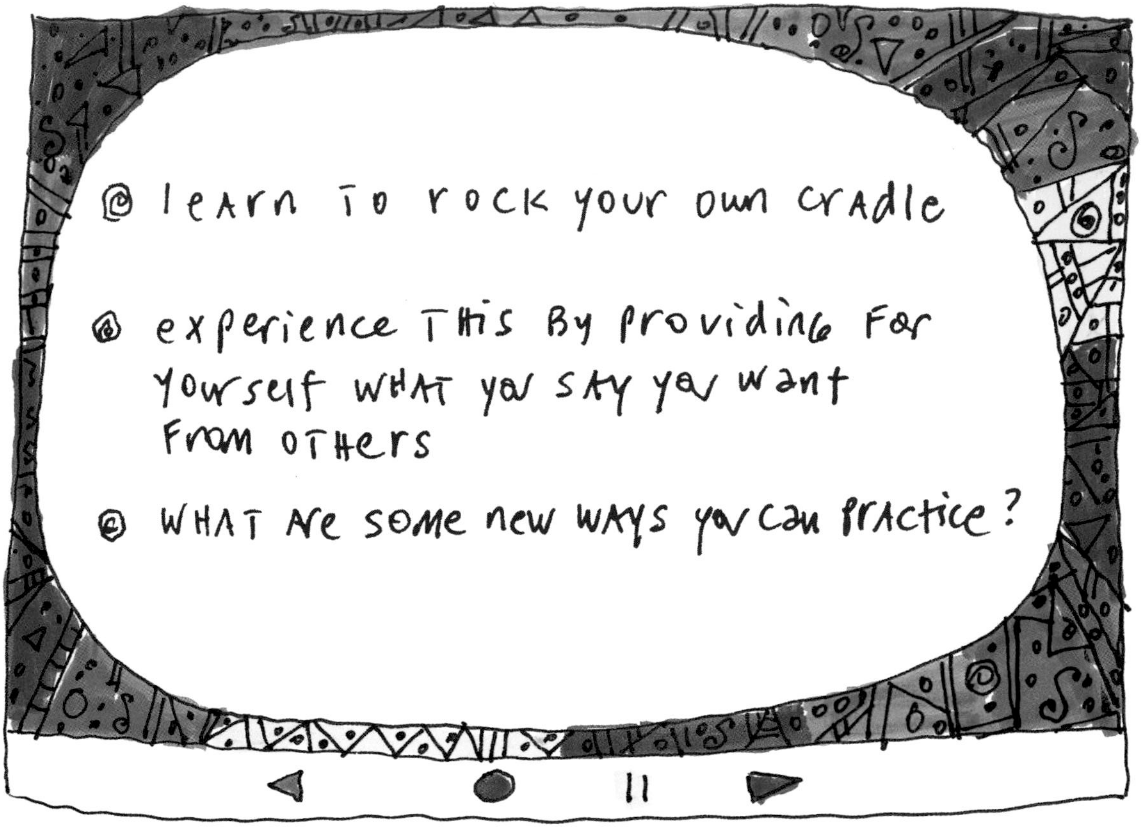

@ leArn To rock your own crAdle

@ experience THis By providing For
yourself WHAT you say you want
From oTHers

@ WHAT Are some new WAYs you can PrActice ?

◀   ●   ‖   ▶

Quotes   For   cHANGe

" Find A plAce inside you wHere
THere is JOY, and THe JOY will
Burn out THe pAin "
JOSepH CAMP Bell

W A V e s
o f
L o v e

"WHO looks outside dreams;
WHo looks inside AWAKes"
CARL JUNG

BOOKS

- Forgive For Love Fred Luskin
- Love is letting Go of Fear Gerald Jampolsky M.D.
- Healing Through The Dark emotions Miriam Greenspan
- I need your love - is That True? Byron Katie
- Choosing me Before we Christine Arylo
- Let Go of The shore Karen Drucker
- Be The person you want To Find Cheri Huber
- Love (luv) n. Karen Porter Sorenson
- Succulent wild woman SARK
- The Art of extreme self-care Cheryl Richardson

web resources

- The work. org
- Abraham-Hicks.com
- Tonic. com
- 1000journalsfilm.com
- Artellaland.com
- Cherylrichardson.com
- emclairepoet.com

MUSIC

- Only BreaTH
Jami sieber + Kim rosen
Jamisieber.com Kimrosen.net

"Failing To Fetch me AT First
Keep encouraged, Missing me one
place search another. I stop
somewhere waiting for you"
WALT WHITMAN

TO
All
THE
CHanGes

WHAT TO DO WITH CHANGE AND LOSSES

Practice Allowing and transforming them.
Remember THAT HEALING and CHANGE HAPPEN in SPIRALS
and lAyers.

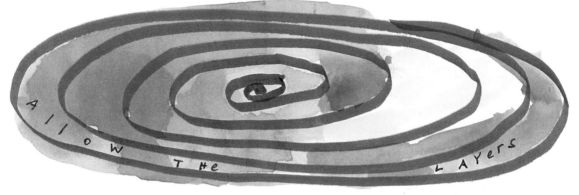

See if you can open your HEART and ARMS TO
WHATever CHANGES HAPPEN and losses occur. I
Sometimes tend to lay A template of the PAST
ONTO THE present and THEN FEEL upset WHEN "THINGS
Are not THE SAME." THEN I start comparing WHAT
USED TO BE TO WHAT is NOT even Known yet and
forget to relax and JUST open Myself to

SOMETHING DIFFerent

Life presents us WITH SO Many CHANCES TO
PRACTICE, BECAUSE it's Constantly CHANGING.
THE opposite of loss is NOT GAIN, it is...found.

WHAT can you FIND WITHin your losses?
I recommend looking For THE GiFTS FiRST.
THEy MiGHT not APPEAr immediately. I'm often
convinced THAT THiS TiME, THEy're JUST. NOT.
THERE. THiS occurs To me in My MiND.

I've learned THAT My MiND is an unreliABle
Guide—By itself. It MAKES uP STories and
repeATS FEArs and resistances. I'M PRACTiCiNG
Allowing My MiND to HAVE some initial input, and
THEN Following My BoDy and emotions to decide
WHAT I ActuALly do, or don't do.

This process looks like deliBerAtely Feeling
My WAy THROUGH THE DAy instead of reHEArsing
and trying to FiGure out "How will it All work?"
DoiNG THiS leAves room for cHANGES and surPrises,
WHICH of course Always occur.

Here's WHAT HAPPENED yesterDAy: My MiND
toLD me to spend THE DAy writing THE BOOK— no
exceptions!

i notice THAT My MiND can Be rATHer
MiLiTARy in its AssiGNMents witH little
reGArD For How I'm ActuALly FeeLiNG

My mind Also toLD me I didn't HAVE TiME
for Feelings. WiTH THiS kind of riGiD MessAGE,

My body and emotions go into revolt. I begin feeling ill and tired, overworked and overwhelmed and quite sorry for myself.

So I asked my body and emotions what they needed and wanted, and listened to what they "said." I then found myself cooking a nourishing meal, cleaning my living space, and calling good friends for support. Several hours later I entered my writing studio with fresh eyes and renewed spirit and started creating what you're reading now.

I realize sometimes there is work to be done that doesn't have as much time or room for contemplation. I do believe that the same inquiry works for those times too — to incorporate our mind, body, and emotions in whatever we're doing.

THERE'S ALWAYS TIME TO FEEL

responses to change and loss

One of my very best change mentors is a multi colored sand painting that is framed and under glass. You can turn it upside down or on its side and the sand moves and changes shape in new, entrancing ways.

It is never the same.

Each time, I'm positive that this one is the best version I've ever seen. I leave it that way for a few hours or days until I am moved to change it again.

Every time, without exception, the new one is as beautifull or more beautifull than what it was before.

This illustrates perfectly how change offers opportunity for our new response.

Sometimes it is not as clear as the sand painting. A few years ago, when my beloved younger brother andrew, made plans to move out of my house where he had lived for a short time, and relocate to Las Vegas, I felt so sad.

I felt sad to not be in close physical proximity anymore and could not imagine how his living in Las Vegas could ever be good.

After my feelings of loss started transforming and changing, I began to feel glad that Andrew was starting a new life in a new city. Friends then pointed out that I'd done the same thing in San Francisco so many years before.

I visited Andrew in Las Vegas and experienced the lower cost of living and ease that Andrew was seeking. I started to accept the change and stopped focusing on "How he used to live here" and "we used to do this." I began also feeling glad for the new things we were doing. Andrew asked me to help him choose a puppy, and OTTO entered the picture with great love and JOY.

I witnessed the changes in Andrew immediately as this unconditional love teacher dog moved into his life and heart. I watched Andrew's heart expanding and changes occurring.

77

Andrew then began experimenting with an online dating service, and after passively seeking and responding to potential dates for some time, he met Jennifer. He and Jennifer visited me in San Francisco, and I liked her immediately and felt very moved when Andrew told me privately:

"I know it's early in our relationship, but I intend to marry her. I've never felt this way about anyone before."

I had the great honor of officiating their wedding ceremony on Dec 27, 2009, and felt astounded to see our family grow with such love. Both Andrew and I received new family members—wife, sister-in-law, and other great in-laws—and I feel like Jennifer's mom, Kathryn, is like a big sister to me.

THESE CHANGES COULDN'T HAVE TAKEN PLACE WITHOUT THE ORIGINAL "loss" of andrew's deparTure. I Guess you COULD say He COULD HAVE MADE THESE SAME CHANGES WHile still LiviNG in San Francisco, But I THINK THAT andrew needed THE cHaNGe To provide THE GrowTH iMpeTus.

Jennifer sHared THAT sHe HAd HAd A BoyFrieNd Before, wHo wHen sHe Got sick and went into THE HospiTal WASN'T THE cAriNG BoyFrieNd sHe HAd wisHed for. So sHe Broke up WiTH Him and FeLT TremeNdous loss duriNG A vvlNerABle Time, aNd woNdered wHo else SHe COULD or wOuLd ever Meet. Two weeks lATer sHe MeT andrew.

I Believe THAT we caN TrusT CHanGe and Give Ourselves time to respond and Feel THe losses, and THen KNOW THAT THE GiFTs Are BeiNG, or will Be, reveAled.

I AM pracTiciNG— Sometimes unwilliNGly, reluctantly, and AT OTHer Times Avidly and wiTH GreAT FAiTH.

Sometimes pAssively, BAdly and GraNdly AvoidiNG

So FAr, THere HASN'T BeeN A SiNGle loss THAT HASN'T sHOwed me SomeTHiNG As Good or even BeTTer THaN wHAT cAme Before. I inteNd to continue experieNciNG THis and iNvite you to JoiN Me.

79

Practicing Allowing Changes

Before my mother died, I asked her what wisdom she would like to pass on. She replied:

"I just wish I hadn't resisted everything so much."

I've taken this wisdom into my heart and life, and have noticed how many times I'm in resistance to, or acceptance of, CHANGE.

So far, it's most often resistance- at least initially

I'm practicing standing in a kind of "neutral middle" when I hear news. For example, when one of my favorite restaurants went out of business, my first reaction was complete resistance.

"WHAT?! you're kidding me. It was always full. They made the best food. I loved bringing people there. This is terrible."

After reacting to and digesting this news, I began to wonder what there could possibly be to be glad about in this situation. Soon after, I heard that the owners were ill and felt so glad to stop working so hard. I started to feel a little glad for them, but still sad for me.

While the restaurant stood empty, I would walk by and fantasize about what else could possibly open there that I would like as much.

Then I forgot all about it, as there were other changes to practice with. One day, I noticed a new restaurant that had opened in the previous space. I felt resistant to the name and the menu, and my mind was so ready to tell me that <u>this time</u> it wasn't as good or better— that it was in fact, worse.

Before I had a chance to try the new restaurant, it also closed and went out of business. I felt relieved.

After awhile, an art gallery opened in that space, and I went in to see a man painting a portrait at the back of the shop. I felt an incredible wave of energy when I saw his face, as though I knew him. We started talking, and I realized that I felt extremely attracted to him...

Wait!

This is actually not true, but it could be! These are the possibilities we close ourselves to when we are so busy resisting.

The space is actually still empty and I've found other delicious new restaurants.

We all have countless stories and examples like this one, and if you begin to consciously practice, whether you're allowing change or resisting change, you'll open up even more avenues of gladness.

As I've described previously, the practice points are in maintaining a kind of neutral middle — where things are neither "bad" or "good," they are just things. We can respond instead of react, be in trust instead of distrust.

The transformations occur when we gather our experiences and remind ourselves of their teaching capacities, and then do the necessary work to change ourselves and our relationship to change.

We can accept the lessons and learn and grow, or resist and disallow the teachings.

It's our choice, and I'm choosing

The
Gladdest
routes

Gifts of Loss and Change

We often forget the gifts and focus instead on what appens to be "missing." I do this frequently when I forget to use my Transformational skills.

One of the Biggest Gifts brought by loss and change is the opportunity to practice:

resiliency

It's easy to talk about being resilient when all is "going well" in our lives. When things are "not going well," we have the choice to respond by accepting or resisting. recently, I was at an airport and informed of a three-hour flight delay. After a moment of resistance, I moved into acceptance and decided to Build a Fort with my velvet cloak and luggage carrier. I then got a bag of cheetos and climbed happily inside my fort. A woman asked if it was a fort and I said in mock defiance, "yes! And you can't come in!"

another gift is:

unconditional love expansion

I was leaving on a trip one time and felt quite ill, so I made myself a sticker that said "please be kind I'm not feeling well" and wore it on my back.

83

I received so many hugs and kind words. One man with a guitar serenaded me. Another woman gave me her neck pillow. My loss of "feeling good" led myself and so many others to change.

Changes and losses lead us to:

WISDOM CHANNELING

We all have a "wise self" inside and can access this wisdom anytime. I speak to "strangers" all the time and utilize this gift. There are lots of tourists in my neighborhood in San Francisco, and recently I noticed several people on top of my hill looking at a map. I asked if I could help, and the woman responded:

"We just want to go somewhere magic and you look like you know magic"

I told her that I did, and that serendipity was everywhere in San Francisco. She got really excited and replied:

"I lost my phone and list of places we were going to go, and then I heard what sounded like my grandmother's voice, but I think it was inside me, telling me to speak to a kind stranger— and I think that's you!"

I complimented her on utilizing her wise self, directed them to all the magic spots I could think of, and introduced myself as SARK... Her exuberant responses would fill another book.

another gift available to us is:

centering ourselves

Whatever is happening to us, or around us, we have the opportunity to practice centering ourselves, and **responding instead of reacting.**

I was at a lavadromat and encountered a violent-acting individual, who was shouting and throwing things. After **experiencing** initial feelings of fear and upset, I centered myself and shouted much louder than him, and kept shouting.

He stopped and stared at me and said, "wow lady. You have a problem."

I smiled at him as he gathered his things and left.

An immense gift I'm receiving and practicing is what I call:

Being Woven and Deepened

I'm learning to get out of what I call the "extremes" of either/or, black/white thinking, and **occupy the rich, fertile middle places.** instead of idealizing or demonizing anything or anyone, I weave [85]

A net in between and deepen my awareness of how everything is a mixture of both. I practice this by noticing when I'm caught in a "polarized spell" of thinking that something is just good or bad, and then living from that place in the middle.

I felt disappointed by a friend recently and began assigning blame and a "sentence" for their mistakes. At these times, I create two lists— one with my complaints, and one where my wise self offers guidance. This results in my being "back in the middle" which is such a great relief.

Having experienced losses and changes allows us to be and have:

increased compassion for self and others

When my mom was in a wheelchair, I felt astounded by how many places were inaccessible and unknowing I'd been to these conditions. I realized that in the past, I used to get impatient at traffic signals if someone was moving slowly.

Now they could crawl across the street, and I would wait patiently and with great love.

We are invited through loss and change to: understand ourselves and others more fully

I USED TO THINK THAT everybody THOUGHT and responded like I do, and now I know THAT THEY can only do AS THEy do, and THINK AS THEY THINK.

I'M continually PRACTICING WITH THIS ONE AS I encounter ALL KINDS if Different people. I've learned THAT THE MORE I understand ABOUT PSYCHOLOGY, THE less I take anything personally.

So I continue To read, study, Attend THERAPY, talk WITH other people ABOUT THEIR experiences, and learn ABOUT MY OWN. THERE Are countless opportunities To PRACTICE! CHANGE and loss Are excellent Mentors For:

expanding Gladness and J O Y

My GrandFATHER told me when I WAS 14:
"Do everything you can THINK of DOING, so you know WHAT you don't Want To do."

I took This literally and HAD Hundreds of JOBS. I discovered SO Many THINGS I didn't Want to do and in THE process discovered so MUCH ABOUT WHAT I DID Want.

My experiences WITH THIS continue, AS I learn THAT WHAT DELIGHTS me MOST, WHAT Brings Me THE Most JOY, is WHAT OTHER People MOST respond TO. every Business loss or CHANGE I've experienced HAS led To an expansion of Gladness and Joy. YEARS AGO, WHEN I WAS creating 87 Hundreds of products, I BEGAN To disLike My own company, which was turning to me to create more Art and words than I could reasonably produce. I now have learned how to create a structure and system for this that works much better. The more good things I notice, the more good things happen to be noticed. And when things happen that I don't like, I know they're just more opportunities to use my transformational skills.

Here's a quick reference guide for you to practice with:

Practice your gifts and opportunities with change and loss in the following ways:

1. Do your Transformational work. So many people try to avoid doing it, and luckily there is no escape.

2. Share your evolving experiences with others. We can all utilize more examples of transformations, and you will benefit by the sharing.

3. Explore your dark or hidden places—you can use a flashlight. This will allow more gladness to flow

4. Allow and participate in Mentoring. We all have things to share with others, and can easily mentor and be mentored without special training.

5. Practice giving and receiving love in new, unfamiliar ways. Experiment with extending yourself in ways you normally don't and receiving what you ordinarily would not. This will open and create new channels for love to flow through

6. Educate others, especially friends and family, in the best ways to support you.

6. (continued) people don't Automatically know. They need to be shown and TAUGHT. This will result in everyone receiving and Living on A "sturdy platform" of support.

7. Become and Live AS A "Full cup of love," Able and willing To share overflow with others
So Many people Live AS A HALF-empty cup, trying To Be Filled By someone or something

8. Tell and Live transformed stories.
So often, we Get into "neGATive story repetition" repeating The same messages and energy Many Times — WAY PAST The point of usefulness.

Welcome and notice The MirAcles and GlADnesses in ALL of it — The Joys, The sADnesses, And All THAT lies in The Middle.

GooD Follows GooD, and The More we notice it, The More shows up!

We reAlly can learn to integrate loss and CHAnGe, infuse ourselves with wisdom, Apply self-love, Liberally and skillfully, investigate and

Allow our Mysteries

and experience The pAins AS well AS The GlADnesses of Life.

"WHAT We HAVe once enjoyed
we can never lose, All
THAT we love deeply Becomes
A PArt of Us "
                    Helen keller

s c r e e n   of c o n t e m p l a t i o n

@ Allow your Joy To leAd

@ experience THis By finding
    WHAT's 6lAd in every cHAnGe

@ PrActice MuLTiplying Joys untiL
    Your cHAnGes Ne Joy-full or will soon
    Become so

Q u o t e s   F o r   c H A n G e

"I MAKe THe Most of All
    THAT comes, and THe
    leAsT of All THAT GoeS "
                    SArA TeAsdAle

To
All
The
Changes

"You can't stop the waves but you can learn how to surf"
Jon Kabat-Zinn

BOOKS

- A Tree Grows in Brooklyn Betty Smith
- Tales of a Wounded Healer Mariah Fenton Gladis
- Forgive for Good Fred Luskin
- Change the Way You See Everything
  Kathryn D. Cramer Ph.D & Hank Wasiak

- What's your Body Telling you? Steve Sisgold
- Seeking Peace Mary Pipher

Web resources

- wounded-healer.com
- esalen.org
- eqi.com
- care2.com
- crazysexylife.com
- robynnola.com

MUSIC

JoshuaKadison.com

"By letting go it all gets done. The world is won by those who let go. But when you try and try, the world is beyond winning"
Lao Tzu

SINGING
THROUGH
THE
STORMS

WHAT'S Good About FALLING To pieces?

While my love relationship was ending, After much grieving, soul searching, therapy and time, I would unexpectedly encounter A new batch of pain and grief.

BECAUSE MOST HEALING happens in spirals and layers, I call this particular version

respiraling

It's when the previous grief re-emerges, or the not-yet-explored places ask for attention. I felt like I was "FALLING TO pieces," which is most of us say when things feel bad, out of control, or desperate in some way.

So often, I try to "keep it together," stay whole, or do <u>ANYTHING</u> but

FALL To pieces

✱ Here's A little piece of me, right here. it just fell off.

I continue to sometimes think of HEALING like marching or CLIMBING and getting to A "Better place" other than the one we're in.

WHEN do we get to FALL APART, get sick, lose our center, or FALL To pieces?

93

It's never convenient.

Avoidance, denial, Busyness all work—in the short term.

What about Just Falling to pieces and Then saying so?

I find that when I can Just speak of it nakedly with no stories or cover-up, it can shift and change.

Whatever "it" is

I'm learning to hold the little hands of those scared parts inside of myself, and Just sit with them.

They love This

This kind of focused attention works to allow instead of deny or resist, and then the pain can loosen or soften.

We all travel to and through these dark and difficult places. We need to Go into the darkness, but I've learned we can use a metaphorical Flashlight when we do. While in the darkness, you can look for other Flashlights and know that you're not alone.*

    * But I'm a private sort of person—an introvert—so this message
    of not Being alone has periodically Felt rather horrifying

I've had profound experiences of "seeing" other dots of light From other Flashlights

I welcome all Flashlights and Fellow dark Travelers!

94

A GreaT deepening can occur in THE DARK

From THE MidsT of "FAlling To pieces:"

- THe pieces reAssemBle
- New pieces MATeriALize
- OLD pieces can Be discarded or reshaped

You find yourself sitting on A pile of dirt, smiling.

I rememBer My former THerapist telling me I looked so Beautifull wHeu I FeLT I WAS FALling to pieces. I THought I looked so UGly.

I THink THAT's Because in THose times we leT THe WAlls down, THe Guards Go Home, THe MAKeup FAlls off and we Are Like

our softest little selves, searching for and finding love, within and witHout

It Feels counterintuitive to Go toward Those Broken, DArk, and Difficult places, But THis is wHere THe Fertile, rich GrowtH TAKes place.

Most GrowtH TAKes place in DArkness

I invite you To FAll to pieces and say so! WeAve A KAleidoscopic cApe From THose pieces and WeAr it To teA!

Share your Discoveries with Fellow travelers

While we were ending/changing our love relationship, I told my former lover I felt like a basket case, and then revised it and said:

"No. I just feel like a basket. I'm not even strong enough to be a basket case."

She replied:

"I'm glad you're a basket, because a basket can be filled. A case is just closed."

Being willing to fall to pieces means:

Crying more, laughing more deeply, and feeling alive in times of primitive pain and disarray.

Here's a little dot of love for you

WHY it's important to Feel our Feelings and WHAT To do WITH THem

Our Feelings Are WITH US All DAY, every dAY, in every moment, yET MAny of US Are oFTen UNAWARE of How we feel.

We judge, Deny, Hide, rePress, inVAliDAte, MiniMize or Try To CHAnGE HOw we ACtUAlly FeeL, in order To "FeeL Better."

OR we love How we FeeL And try To CLinG To THOSe FeeLinGs To "MAKe THem lAsT," And GeT More of THOSe "Good" FeelinGS.

FeelinGs THemselves don't cNre About any of THis— THey JUST Keep on Feeling, no MATter WHAT else is HAppening, or How we MiGHT Be trying to SHAPe or ControL THem.

If we don't Allow ourselves To FeeL or express our eMotions, THey will GeT lNrGer or louder or MAy Go into our Bodies And present THemselves As some kind of PHysicAL condition.

FeelinGs Are MeAnt To Be in Motion. e · MOTion. FeelinGs Are MADe To Be expressed. You've proBABly HeArd: "If you cAn FeeL it, you can HeAl it." And THis is Trve—yet MAny try To STop FeelinG Before THe HeAling TAKes plAce, especially if it seems Like A "BAd" or DiFFicvLt Feeling.

97

As soon as a "bad" feeling dissipates, we run to the next, better feeling and forget to do our **practices of transformation**, where we simply allow the feeling, whatever it is, and Feel it before trying to move to move to the next feeling.

I notice that when I clamber out of a bad-feeling place, I become convinced that it will never occur again.

Of course it does, and I'm almost just as surprised as the first time

Luckily, experience is showing me that I can count on feeling that bad again, and this actually good because when it occurs, I have my transformative tools ready.

My friend eLissa was listening to some of my sad feelings when my lover relationship was ending, and she said:

"I'm so glad you can Feel this."

And I asked "Why??" through my tears.

She replied, "Since you're able to feel this much pain, you can feel this much joy. Many people don't allow the feelings and consequently numb themselves to feeling much of anything. I know you wouldn't want that. I also want you to know, in case you've temporarily forgotten, that you are more than your sadness. You're able to have other feelings in between, and it's not all that you are, or all of your experience."

This felt like tremendous relief—I felt so gratefull to be seen by her and witnessed in my experience. And since I had fallen into a pit of sadness, I was particularly happy to hear and feel her viewpoint. Because I had temporarily become convinced that I would or could feel only sadness for the rest of time.

In the midst of strong emotions, I can also feel very dramatic and extreme. When this happens, I know I have left my transformative practice work and reoccupied the

extremes

In the extremes, drama and intensity are required and rewarded. everything is either bad or good, glad or mad, white or black.

There is no middle

From the extremes, feelings have no nuance or subtlety; they are just

This
or
That

and are often very loud and playing all at once. So you can't hear the individual feelings or notes in between.

From the middle place, I can feel things like: relief, weariness, wistfulness, longing, yearning, tiny hope, miniature gladness, grateful collapse, willing resistance and sad happiness.

When we nurture ourselves and practice in the middle places, we can expand our feeling capacities greatly and increase our range of e-motion.

Some might wonder if all these feelings are "too much" or "too many." I know I sometimes fear being consumed by them. I'm learning that the more I can actually feel my feelings, whatever they are, the less time I actually need to spend feeling! I used to spend so much time and energy resisting my feelings, or trying to rewrite them, that I wasn't just living and feeling them.

Now that I am, I don't think about it as much. I just feel whatever it is and keep flowing to the next feeling.

and sometimes flowing looks more like trickling

I'm learning to trust that no feeling lasts forever and there are always more feelings to feel - in fact, an endless supply, no scarcity!

100

Here are some things to try and experience
with your feelings:

@ AWARENESS
How do you FEEL? do you know? See if you
can describe the feeling(s) See if there are more
than one. Write down or speak your feelings
out loud. START PRACTICING MAKING notes about
your feelings—maybe in your JOURNAL. I sometimes
practice while WALKING, saying feelings out loud
until they change into the next one.

@ Allowing
Letting your FEELINGS HAVE A place is to
Allow THEM to (BE). WHEN we can Allow THEM To
Be, THEy can Transform into new ones. WHEN we
can practice not ATTACHING Meaning To our
FEELINGS THEy can just exist AS THEy Are, AS
WE Are. See if you can practice Allowing whatever
FEELING(s) you Are experiencing right now. If not,
Just Allow THAT too.
HOLD THE Hand of whatever feeling it is. Just sit and HOLD Hands. Allow it.

@ ALCHEMY
To "ALCHEMIZE" Means to Modify, CHange THE
SHApe if, or TransMute. Once you've practiced BEING AWAre
of your feelings and Allowing THem. You MAy wish TO
experiment with some ALCHEMY. We can Assist our
FEELINGS Along THE WAY. Sometimes feelings can Get stuck

in negative repetition or our beliefs about those feelings. This is different than the feelings themselves. For example, we might keep saying we feel grief, and forget that we are woven through with joy, or grace, or primitive sadness. The more descriptive language we can develop and use with our feelings, the more we can soften and change with those feelings, and the feelings can change shape.

@ Support

Most feelings love to be heard, witnessed and seen. Some feelings feel more private or primitive or more difficult to describe. As you do your transformative practices and feelings experiments, you will benefit from having support. This support is in this book, in other books, online, or by phone, or you may wish to ask another person to join you. This person and you can have a feelings check-in process, where you each say how you feel, with no solutions or judgments, just allowing and witnessing. You may wish to describe your feelings in more detail or ask for feedback. Develop a "feelings language" and shorthand for how you feel. Learn about others' feelings and how common yours are. Be reminded that there are no linear measurements of feelings and stop "trying to feel better."

Practice stopping describing feelings in extremes and supporting other people in doing this. Introduce the middle way you're practicing to others and invite them to join you.

@ Transformation

As you become more experienced with feeling your feelings, you can practice transforming them. You will start to be able to tell when you've felt a feeling "long enough" and can allow it to transform.

* Be cautious about trying this too soon without actually feeling your feelings— especially if they're uncomfortable ones

I've discovered that it's easiest to transform each feeling into a similar, slightly less uncomfortable one— from mad to upset, upset to worried, worried to curious— rather than trying to go straight from mad to curious.

I often have dreams related to what I'm writing about and recently dreamed that I watched a black cat fall off a tall building. I ran down to try to help the cat and felt amazed that it wasn't lying there in a heap, crushed by the fall. Instead I saw it calmly sitting to the side watching me. I exclaimed out

loud: "How did you _do_ THAT?"
And THE CAT smiled slightly and said:

"Don't you know we all have wings?"

I think our AWAreness of feelings gives us our wings. The more we can feel, the more we will be able to FLOW, SOAr, Dive, Leap, Crawl, and lie still...

... Just Breathing and...
Feeling
and
Transforming.

STAY WITH YOURSELF IN TIMES OF STRONG EMOTION

WHEN EXPERIENCING STRONG EMOTIONS, ITS very TEMPTING TO ABANDON OURSELVES, TO DO ANYTHING TO GET AWAY FROM WHAT HURTS.

If you practice STAYING WITH YOURSELF AT SUCH TIMES, YOU'LL BE CREATING A FOUNDATION OF STRENGTH THAT NO LOSS, DEATH, OR CHANGE CAN SHAKE.

AND EVEN WHEN IT DOES SHAKE, YOU WON'T MIND AS MUCH

Here ARE SOME WAYS TO PRACTICE STAYING WITH YOURSELF:

@ identify
YOUR STRONG EMOTIONS. WRITE THEM DOWN, NAME THEM, GIVE DESCRIPTIONS, CONSIDER USING COLLAGE OR ART

@ experience
THE SENSATIONS STRONG EMOTIONS BRING UP IN YOUR BODY. BECOME AWARE OF WHERE THEY SHOW UP AND DETAIL IN WRITING OR AUDIO - HOW IT FEELS PHYSICALLY

@ practice
SKILLFULLY DECIDING WHETHER TO EXPERIENCE YOUR FEELINGS BY YOURSELF OR WHETHER AND HOW TO SHARE THEM WITH OTHERS. IF SHARING WITH OTHERS, CAREFULLY CHOOSE KINDRED SPIRITS WHO CAN HOLD YOUR FEELINGS WITH YOU AND NOT JUDGE THEM - OR CHOOSE A THERAPEUTIC ADVISOR.

@express

your strong emotions in some way, whether through sharing, art, physical movement like dance, or breaking something. For example: I recycled a cat toy after the toy part fell off, and a flexible stick remained. I use the stick part to whip recycled paper bags until they're shredded to ribbons.

By staying with your strong emotions and practicing in these ways, you can become much more willing to be present for yourself and for others.

Through practicing these processes, you will spend less time resisting or trying to escape strong emotions, and by feeling and living through them, you will experience your strength and capacities you didn't even know you had.

remember
THAT emotions flow when we
can feel them, and they
get stuck when we don't, or can't

By staying with yourself in the midst of your feelings, you will develop a strong, benevolent presence who can hold you through any emotional storm.

You can Also practice Briefly, BAdly,
or unknowingly, and it will still "work."

Allow
Most of All!

Allow any messy, tortured feelings
and KNOW THAT THey Are SHiFtiNG and CHANGING
By THe instant.

No FeeliNG LAsts Forever

Allowing your feeliNGs works

How incredible and Resilient we are
* especially when we don't feel that way

In my life and glad practices, I'm continually astounded by people and their strength and resiliency.

During a recent workshop I facilitated, people shared these experiences:

⊙ A woman who had had multiple brain surgeries for recurring tumors allowed people to feel the scars on her head and everyone bonded together at the fragility of life.

⊙ A man who arrived wearing a dark baseball cap and cloud of sadness shared that he had just emerged from a long period of depression and felt ready to shift—and did.

⊙ A woman whose husband has dementia and can't be left alone for too long shared that her husband had encouraged her to stay the whole weekend for the workshop and not drive back and forth.

⊙ A woman who writes beautiful books and had begun feeling that her writing was just too much work had a revelation that she could be liberated in joy with her writing—and then experienced it.

We ALL HAVe periods of lonely FeArs, or PAinfUL Shynesses, MULTiple Kinds of anxieties, Frustrations, losses, and experiences of broken or elusive Dreams.

We ALso HAVe GreAT Hopes, illuMinATions, revelations, creATive commitMent, and certAinty of our dreAms.

even in THe midsT of THe lArGe eARTHQuAKe in HAiti, people sHow THis resiliency of spirit. A HAitian Actor THere To Help sAid,

> "Don't worry About THe HAitians—
> we HAVe THe HeArTs of Lions"

THis resilient spirit continves despite All sorts of circumstances. even when it AppeArs THAT someone or someTHinG is crusHed, THere is Always renewAl.

People AMAze me, over and over. THey pick up THeir dreAms and Keep MoVinG, no MAtter WHAT THe losses and cHanGes.

_We still sHow up.

In THAT sHowing up, energies sHiFt and Flow and transform. Over and over, FACiLTATinG workshops, I see people Arrive WiTH some version of 109

OTHers can Do it and not me
and leave with
OTHers can do it and so can I !
And THe strongest inspirations I've ever
found Are

    JOY
    Love
    DeLiGHT

We Are AWaKened By JOY

escorted By Love

Driven By DeLiGHT
            and
G L A D Follows GLAD
    We can Also do These Transformative
Glad practices for ourselves By reading BOOKS,
ASKING Friends To Mentor us, and creATing TriBes
of support. I see THAT we Frequently overestimate
our FeArs and underestimate our STrenGTHS.
    If we "interview" our Friends and closest 110

supporters and ASK THem TO speak of our STRENGTHS, we would HeAr A List of Glowing words and observations.

We can Also create A List like THis for ourselves and PAper our WALLs WiTH it

I AM SO Brave and Kind and Big Hearted

THese SAme Friends and supporters Also see our "splendid imperfections," FLAWS, FAILINGS, WeAKnesses, pLAces of collApse and resistance.

WHen we do our Transformative practices and Listen wiTH love, we can practice HOLDING All The pArts, For and wiTH our loved ones — THe STrenGTHS and WEAKnesses and everyThing in Between. This of course leAds to consistently doing it For ourselves.

BecAuse we Are WHole, HUMAn and MAde up of everyThing:

SOLID, rAttly, lost, Asleep, AWAKened, MUMBLInG, sinGinG, Hiding, DespAiring, CrAWLInG, leApinG, creATinG, resistinG, openinG, loving, leAving, closinG, Hoping

L i v i n G.

A WHole universe of GlAd, sAd and in Between.

And it isn't necessary to FeeL strong To Be stronG. THe vision creates THe strenGTH.

eMotional GPS

I BOUGHT A GPS (wHicH I THiNK stands for "Good
POiNTiNG system") A FeW YeArs AGO, As I WAS one of
THoSe "directionally cHallenGed" people in A cAr. As A
WilDly iMAGiNATive visual ArtisT, I see every route
Completely Differently eAcH Time, no MATTer tHow MAny
Times I've driven it.
             I used to drive Around A lot, losT and crying

THe GPs HAs Assisted me tremendously in discovering
aud GoinG To new places. My BroTHer andrew initially
worried I woulD Grow dependent on it, and I woulD
Feel really losT if iT Broke or stopped functioning.

Actually, THe opposite HAs occurred. THe More
I see THAT THere Are really Actual routes To and From
places, and THe GPs finds THem, THe More confident I
Feel THAT I can and will find THem too. I've Become More
exploratory and experimental in My nAviGATing of roAds and
HiGH wAys, and HAVE Also BeneFited GreATly From THe "recAlculATing"
FeATure of THe GPs—wHere it DetecTs A Difference in
THe route TAKen, and an AutomATed voice sAys,
"recAlculATing," unTil it delivers THe revised route.

I 've tAKen THis system and Applied
      it To My eMotional Life Also

112

For example, if I'm BLAMING or COMPLAINING or ACTING out in some WAY, I will MUTTER "**RECALCULATING**" TO MYSELF and CHOOSE A new emotionAL route.

If DIFFICULT or destructive FEELINGS persist, I keep recalculating until I've discovered A Different WAY TO GO. This works especially well if I'm "in reaction" TO another person and WHAT FEELINGS THEY'VE AWAKENED in me.

MY emotionAL GPS Allows me TO CHANGE **reactions** TO **responses,** which ARE often EASIER TO NAVIGATE and MANAGE.

In response Mode, I'm USUALLY ABLE TO MAINTAIN SOME emotionAL OBJECTIVITY, SHARE FEELINGS SAFELY and FAIRLY, and "OWN" MY experience instead of SHOVELING it All onto another person in reactivity.

While AT The BANK recently, I WAS HANDLING The THEFT of MY credit cArd number and MULTIPLE FRAUDULENT CHARGES THAT HAD HAPPENED AFTER I'd instructed The BANK to cancel The cArd and THEY HADN'T done it. I SAT WITH The BANK officer AFTER BEING TOLD of THIS, and BLURTED out:

"I JUST FEEL SO irrationally angry!
I know it isn't your FAULT—you weren't The person WHO WAS supposed to cancel The cArd—BUT you're The person sitting Here. THANK you For listening To me."

113

She thanked me for acting responsibly with my feelings, and shared with me that most people don't.

Most people don't know how

As she yellow-highlighted all the changes that I would need to fill out paperwork about and get affadavits for, I exclaimed:

"This isn't FAIR! I feel cheated and made to do work because of this criminal and the bank's mistake."

She validated my feelings and apologized for the frustrations and then leaned over and said:

"I would feel exactly the same way. I am honoring your feelings and respect your right to feel them!"

With her statement and great response, my emotional GPS calculated a new route and I left the bank resolved in the situation. I've forgiven the bank and the criminal and am not repeating the blaming, angry stories but instead the recalculated-route stories of resolution and redemption.

We all have access to an emotional GPS within and can utilize our transformative practices and skills to support feeling our feelings, create new routes, and tell new stories.

"WHen we Are unABle to find trAnQuiLity
WiTHin ourselves,
it is vseless to seek it elsewHere"

Core-A-te

screen   of   contemplation

@ mArry your riGHt and left BrAins

@ Do THis By recALibrATinG your eMotionAL
and THinKinG styles into A Blended operAtion

@ Find yourself "livinG in THe middle" very
STronG, very centered

Qvotes   For   cHAnGe

"THe winds of GrAce Are
Blowing, it is you wHo must rAise
Your sAils"

TAGore

SINGING
THROUGH
THE
STORMS

"Every loss in Life I
consider as the throwing
off of an old garment in
order to put on a new one;
and the new garment has
always been better than
the old one"
HAZRAT INAYAT KHAN

BOOKS

⊚ loving WHAT is Byron Katie
⊚ emotional alchemy TARA Bennett-Goleman
⊚ I HAD it All THE TiMe Alan cohen
⊚ NO enemies within DAWNA MARKOVA
⊚ plan B anne Lamott
⊚ The astonishing power of emotions
                Esther and Jerry Hicks
⊚ THE BODACIOUS BOOK of succulence SARK

web resources

⊚ JOY2Mev. com/emotions
⊚ Goodgrief. org
⊚ Freewillastrology. com
⊚ WAKeupcaHcOacH. com
⊚ Dailyom. com
⊚ DREAMToHEAL ·com
⊚ Hellogrief. com
⊚ Alancohen. com

MVSiC

Let it Be
SUNG BY CAROL WOODS

"Our Heads are round
So our THOUGHTS can
CHANGE Direction"
FRancis PICABIA

leArning
TO
see
in
THe DArK

Learning and practicing seeing in the Dark

Experiencing DEATH in your Life is an opportunity to learn to see in the DARK. It's UNFAMILIAR, it seems IMPOSSIBLE, and you MAY BUMP your knees while moving forward. Other people can't see in the DARK either.

If you say:

"My Mother died"

The first questions will usually be:

"HOW OLD WAS SHe?"

"WAS SHe SICK?"

If she was old and sick, people will usually offer brief words of comfort and then quickly move on from the subject. If she was younger and HEALTHier, people will spend a little more time comforting, then quickly move on from the subject.

Most people Think or say:

"I don't know what to say or do, or how to help!"

Why do we forget that kindness and simple attention always works?

People also say:

"I'm Afraid To say THe wrong THing."

SAYING NO THING is definitely the wrong thing.

Asking how old someone was or whether they were ill is not wrong; it's just misguided if you stop there. There are kind questions to ask and meaningful things to say. At the end of the chapter, I'll provide some suggestions.

We try to hide from death or not speak of it, as though it's contagious. People speak in hushed tones. Children are kept away from

The Sadness

After death, we often wear black, we cry, we might eat too much or too little, we say:

"At least he (or she) didn't suffer."

or

"Thank heavens the suffering is over."

"We can only hope the suffering will end soon."

We're as terrified of suffering as we are of grieving. We often try to decide what suffering is for another person. When I helped to take care of my mother for several years toward the end of her life, she was in and out of hospitals and nursing homes a lot. People had decided she was "suffering" and stopped visiting her.

Often, my mother was playing cards and drinking root beer floats, but it had been decided that she was

Suffering

And therefore, not available.

Her friends had noticed that her lifestyle and mobility had changed, and many stayed away because they couldn't stand to see her "suffer."

We might say:

"Poor _____. She used to get out and _____. Now we never see her anymore.

We forget or don't realize that part of someone's suffering could be alleviated by compassionate attention, and that further suffering is often caused by the people who say they don't want someone to suffer!

They'll say:

"I just can't stand to see _____ like that."

I think that we need to be very clear about what suffering is, and isn't, and cultivate ways to manage our own feelings about it. When we go to a foreign country, we often get a guide book, to learn about the customs, money, and places to see.

Death and grief can be like a foreign country. If we are forced to go, we don't want to stay at all or to stay too long.

120

Allow This BOOK to be your foreign country guidebook to show you the gladnesses and gifts of grief and loss, and the particular ways to make it a good place to travel to. One of the gifts I received after my father died was the ability to be much closer to his spirit. Our "personality selves" had clashed, and his death opened the way for different kinds of spiritual communications to take place.

One of the many gifts I experienced when my mother died was a clear view of how much she had really supported me in my life. I hadn't been able to see how much while she was alive. Now I also see that support for myself is inside me, and that I learned it from her.

The main gift from my cat's death was the unconditional love we shared, and that I experienced myself as being able to selflessly give to another. I am incorporating that gift into my human relationships now.

Experiencing the "gifts of death" is not being disrespectful of, or avoiding being sad. It is an addition to the sadness.

The sadness and gladness are intertwined.

People often try to rush the process of grieving. If we think that someone is grieving "too much" we want to get them out of it and into a "better place."

Time moves in seconds and seasons in grieving.

First, you move second by second, not sure how you'll keep breathing. Next, you look up to see that spring has arrived.

No one can say what another's grief journey should be or needs to be.

When Elisabeth Kübler-Ross wrote about the stages of grief, it was an immensely helpful map. denial · anger · bargaining · depression · acceptance

We need to remember that those stages are NOT linear; they don't happen in order— instead they are circular and recurring.

Yes, life goes on after death, as it does and must. The grieving person, too, goes on in their grief and life. I felt so glad when I spoke to one of the hospice care workers who attended the death of my mother, Marjorie. She said: "You can be really glad for your mom. She was so bold in her death, so bold."

My goddaughter Vanessa told me I was "magnificent in my grief." I asked her what she meant. She said:

"You are just glowing with life."

GIFTS of DEATH
(spells God)

I spent so many years fearing Death that it feels like living in an Alternate universe to be able to experience the gifts of Death now. Through the Deaths of friends, my parents, and my cat, I've experienced profound transformations and received messages about what death is, and isn't.

Perhaps the biggest gift I've received is the awareness that

Death is all right

Every dead person has communicated this to me, through dream states, direct messages, symbols and other "paranormal" experiences.

I believe that we all have the ability to communicate with dead people—some people just don't want to. Some people believe that only "experts" can, and don't even try.

The gifts of Death will appear whether we do or don't choose to communicate with the dead. I have this theory that all the dead people are gathered somewhere, observing the living people and saying things like:

"Oh, look, they're still sad. Don't they KNOW what happens?"

We Are conditioned TO THINK THAT DeATH is BAD, Life is Good. And THAT deATH MUST Be FOUGHT aud BATtled AGAINST, THAT Life is Better.

Life is not Better, it's Just Different

THese polarized opposites: BAd/Good, win/lose, Better/worse consistently leave out THe Middle— WHere JOY Lives Alongside SADness, HUMor exists During DeATH, aud MUltiple feelings Abound.

My MOTHer's DeATH Provided me WiTH so Many GiFTS. SHe WAS A very stubborn forMer MArine WHO resisted deATH As fiercely As SHe HAD Lived Life. I NAMed Her "MArvelous MArjorie" AFter profiling Her in My BOOK Succulent wild WOMan. SHe would Quickly tell people:

"My dAVGHTer NAMed me THAT. I didn't do it."

in THe MidWest WHere SHe lived, THese Kinds of "self-centered" references Are frowned upon, or just not done

Over THe years SHe completely Adopted THe NAMe aud Grew To love it. Some of Her MAiL WAS Addressed TO JUST "MArvelous."

During Her THree-year dying process aud HeALTH CHAllenges, SHe refused To cHange Most of Her HABits THAT MiGHT HAve resulted in Her Living longer.

124

My brother Andrew and I just eventually surrendered to her will and wishes, and just loved her as much as we could.

We learned so much about letting go and our supreme lack of control over our mother's life.

I learned that I could safety-pin myself to her body, hire the top doctors, nutritionists, cooks, and caregivers, and I still

COULDN'T SAVE HER
or
Prevent her DEATH

It seems obvious that I would know that this was true, but certain aspects of myself were like some kind of misguided version of Hercules, convincing me that if I just did enough of the <u>right things</u> at the <u>right times</u> I could prolong or maybe even save her life.

Then there were the opportunities for GUILT, which dotted my inner landscape and appeared in dreams. The theme felt nearly constant:

I WASN'T DOING ENOUGH

No matter how many books I read or people I talked with about **caregiver's guilt** or burnout, or any other sensible advice I received, I still felt guilt because it was my mom.

And, if I felt I wasn't doing enough, it became compounded when I realized that Andrew and I were doing it

imperfectly

We didn't hire a care manager soon enough. We hired inferior caregivers. We didn't monitor her health issues closely enough. We didn't visit, call, or write often enough or live close enough.

We couldn't convince her to move to be near us

None of the above came from her, by the way. This guilt was all self-induced. She was glad to receive whatever my brother and I had to give.

I overfunctioned, hovered, worried, micromanaged and lived in a certain kind of ambient despair.

By now you're probably wondering what or where the gifts are!

The gifts were and are:
- That I lived through it!
- Learning that I could consistently show up and care for someone I loved

- Being given the opportunity to creatively manage my mother's care and be trusted to have power of attorney and health care directive
- Finding strengths and resources I didn't know I had, and continuing to utilize them today—including working with a mentor   Thank you Patricia!
- THAT THE FEARS I HAD of Her <u>ever</u> DYING were eclipsed by Her ACTUAL DEATH
- That the pregrieving I'd done for years had absolutely no effect on my feelings when she died. But who knows how it may have helped along the way?
- Learning to receive help and assistance from others   <u>So</u> many miracles and miraculous people

I was able to provide so many delight-full things to my mom during her time in nursing homes. One remarkable gift continues to nourish me today when I think of it.

She was in a nursing home with bad lighting and bare walls. I brought in floor lamps, music, and a rainbow suncatcher to hang in her window. I created posters and affirmations for the walls and then got inspired to reach out to my readers and ask if anyone felt like sending her a card or note, and gave the nursing home address.

AT FIRST MY MOM WAS SLIGHTLY HORRIFIED, and SAID:

"WHY ARE THESE people writing to me? THEY dont even know me!"

I explained THAT THEY knew HER THROUGH me and MY BOOKS. BY THE next week SHE WAS SAYING:

"I GOT cards and letters FROM england, AUSTRALIA and New zealand TODAY! let me SHOW you."

As THE CARDS and letters STREAMED in, we Filled HER WAlls WITH THEM. THE oTHer residents in THE nursing HOME WOULD LiNe up DAily TO come into HER room and read THE new ones. THOUSANDS of cARds and letters CAME and kept coMiNG.

I continue to Feel GrateFull to every person WHO Wrote OR THOUGHT Nbout writing.

I received A remarkable GIFT FROM my MoTHer in THe lastyear of Her Life. It WAS A Gift of words, and sHe made A point To say to me:

"I Know THAT you're doing Absolutely everyTHING THAT you can For me, and you're doing it All perfectly, and I AM SO GrateFull."

SHe HAd often spoken very criticAlly To me, and I FelT Astonished By THis GIFT. even THOUGH I WOULD HAVE provided THe same cAre anyWAY, it FelT so incredibly nourishing TO HeAr. SHe told me lATer it's WHAT SHe wished Her MoTHer would HAVe said To Her, so she made sure To say it To me.

128

We all have the opportunity to take something that previously hurt us and turn it into a gift for someone else.

For some reason, I always knew that my mother would want to die alone, without her friends or family near. I know that people design and orchestrate their deaths, and I trusted her choice to die in this way.

I think that many people fear dying alone, and in fact, I think we glorify dying in the presence of others as though it is "better" or more evolved somehow.

So often, the best description we can think of about death are "peacefull and with family and friends at the bedside," which is absolutely great for people who wish this.

I havent died yet (that I can consciously recall), but I'm pretty sure that I'll choose to die differently than surrounded by people and know that others feel this way too.

As a private sort of introvert, I envision it differently

I'd been invited to officiate my friends' wedding in Italy, and tried to talk delicately to my mom about my going. I forgot that she wasnt a delicate person, and I finally blurted out:

"I'm afraid you'll die when I'm not here!"
To which she calmly replied:

"Well, I'd be just as dead if you were here! You have to go to that wedding—and I want to hear all the details."

Italy and the wedding were like a dream— a villa outside Lucca in Tuscany, doves flying, an Italian interpreter, and my dear friends Jennifer and Paolo and their families.

My mom did get to hear all the delicious details, but the next day, I got a call saying she wasn't "doing well." After 3 years of witnessing different versions of her not doing well, I'd gotten kind of blunt, and just finally said, "Well, is she dying?"

The hospice worker assured me that she was. "She hasn't spoken in over 11 hours. She hasn't eaten or had anything to drink. Her internal organs are shutting down."

I asked her to hold the phone up to my mother's ear and said,

Hi, Mom, this is Susan."
My mother's loud, booming, completely normal-sounding voice responded:

"Hi Susan!"

I knew immediately THAT SHE WAS inside
Herself in THere, HiDing From THe Hospice workers.
    So I ASKed:
    "Mom, Do you THink you're Dying?"
    and she responded loudly:
    "OH, THis isn't serious!"
I told Her WHAT THe Hospice workers HAd told
Me ABout Her organs shutting down, and There WAS
A long pause, and THen she said softly:
    "I love you susan."
    I knew THen THAT SHE knew SHE WAS
Dying and told Her I WAS on My WAY BACK From
Italy. AT THAT point My international cell pHone
died and I turned To THe pHone in THe ApArtMeut
I WAS staying AT.
    It took A wHile to Get someone To answer
THe pHone AT 5 AM and come Get me to Go to
THe Airport—especially since I don't speAK Italian.
    THen THe driver didn't speAK english, and
WHen I told Her THAT My MoTHer HAd died, SHe
took it to MeAn THAT I wanted to Go to A cHurch
to prAy for Her. So After A wild ride THrough
Marrow coBBlestone streets, we pulled up To
A cHurch! I yelled "Aeropuerto" and we ended
up Arriving late for My FLIGHT. WHen I Got To THe
Counter, THe ticket Agent Handed me A note THAT said:

131

"Our airport is broken.
You will need to take a bus
to another city."

The agent told me that if I hurried, I could get
the last seat on the bus. I ran through a thunderstorm
and just barely made it. As I sat down, the sky
cleared and sun streamed in through the bus window.

I knew in that moment that my mom
had already died. Then the supposedly out-of-battery
cell phone rang, and it was my brother Andrew telling
me that she had died.

The bus pulled out, and I sat surrounded
by strangers who didn't speak English for the next several
hours as we drove through the Italian countryside.

Through my tears, I looked out the window
to see that the world was really "rolling out the beauty."
I felt so aware that my mother was now free
to be a part of everything, and I saw her spirit
in birds flying up to the bus windows, fields of
wildflowers, waterfalls, and groves of flowering
trees.

I cried so hard all the blood vessels in my
eyes broke. I cried openly without restraint, and
kind people spoke to me, made me tea, wrapped me
in blankets for the long flight across the Atlantic.

When I arrived in Minneapolis, my brother
Andrew said, "It's really sad at her house, the

132

Hospital Bed is still Here."

I said, "we're not staying There. I had a vision that we would go to a luxury Hotel."

Andrew expressed some concerns, which I overrode, and soon we were ensconced in a suite, and He was in a long marble bathtub watching Star Trek on a TV screen at the end of it. I Heard Him Through the door saying.

"I am so glad you thought of this."

We slept for Hours, went swimming and gathered our energies for the funeral Home and Service at the Church.

At The Funeral Home Andrew and I Held Hands and stood at Her casket to say our goodbyes to Her Physical body. We Had chosen not to Have Her body embalmed, and as we looked into The casket at Her, one of Her eyes popped open! We gasped and started laughing That even in death, she was "watching" us. In Practical terms, The glue Had come loose.

Our Mother Had always Hated less-than-direct descriptions for death, and God Help anyone who said something like "passed away" in Her presence.

At The Funeral, Andrew gave his talk and said in it: "Some of you know That our Mother Hated euphemisms for death. So if you attempt to console us about our Mother "passing away" we will be forced to correct you by saying that she _died_."

All the people attending went out of their way not to say "passed away," sometimes stopping in midsentence to correct themselves.

We asked the organist to play one of her favorite songs in a very lively fashion, since our mother disliked dirge-like organ music. We were all immensely entertained by a rousing version of "You Are My Sunshine."

Our older brother, Roger, appeared from his homeless alcoholic haze, in a badly fitting borrowed suit, smelling of alcohol and body odor, saying random wild things. We felt scared and uncomfortable having him there, but agreed we needed to let him speak.

We were all holding our breath as he stood up at the front of the church. He said:

"My name is Roger. I'm the black sheep of the family. But I'm here because of my mom. She was a good mom and I loved her. I'll miss her so much."

We all cried and applauded with relief and amazement. I read my poster "Just For Mom" and had a lot of difficulty speaking through my tears. One of my mother's caregivers attended the funeral

WITH MY MOM'S LITTLE yorkie dOG THAT SHE HAD
ASKed if SHE COULD Bring. Our Mom HAD ADored
Her dOG, so we SAid: "Yes, pleASe!"

AFter THe funerAL, A Man cAme up to me and
SAid:

"I need to tell you someTHING, and I'm reAlly
SHook up ABout it. I'M an enGineer, and noTHING
Like THis HAS ever HAppened To me."

I encourAGed Him To continue.

"DUring THe service, I looked over AT THAT
Yorkie dOG THAT WOMAN WAS HOLDING, and I
SAw your Mom's eyes inside THe DOG's eyes!"

I lAVGHed and SAid:

"of course you did! THAT'S JUST WHere My
Mom WOULD SHow up. Don't worry A All if it's
hot loGicAL."

He went AwAy SHAKING His HeAd and
Muttering.
He's new To THE PARANORMAL reALMS

Since our MOTHer HAd Been A MArine, SHe WAS
BUried in A MILiTAry cemetAry. We HAD WAnted to put
"MArvelous MArjorie" on Her tomBstone, and SHe'd
WAnted it too. Before SHe died, I inquired and WAS
toLD THAT no nickNAmes were Allowed, no exceptions.
I wrote numerous letters Trying To HAve THis
CHanGed, To NO AVAiL.

135

A year after she died, I visited Minneapolis and went to finally see the tombstone, which hadn't been ready when she was buried.

I also wanted to see my parents' tombstones and graves "together." I arrived very early in the morning before catching my flight back to San Francisco and realized that I had no idea where my parents' graves were in this huge military cemetary, and the office was closed.

I started to cry and felt so terrible that I literally couldn't find my dead parents. In complete despair, I decided to try channeling the spirit of my dead mother, who had always been very good with maps and directions and could never understand why I wasn't.

I sat in my rental car waiting for some kind of guidance, and then I heard my mother's voice so clearly:

"Susan. Drive straight to the top of that hill and take a right. Just past that row of trees is where your father and I are buried."

I drove slowly, barely able to believe what I was hearing. There by those trees were my parents' graves. I felt so happy to find them, I lay down in the middle between them, and just started laughing and crying and talking with them, just like I used to when they were alive.

THen I SAW my Mom's tombstone and WHAT WAS
Written on it. It said:

MARvelous MARGe

THey HAd SHortened Her NAMe, But sHe loved THe
NAMe MARGe too! I Felt so AMAZed AT THis GiFT,
THis incredible GiFT. So I used my purple pen and
BACK of THe cemetary MAP to MAKe THis TRACiNG:

We never found out WHo MAde THe exception, But we THANK THem

I don't plan To HAve A toMBstone But if
I did, it WouLD SAY Just one word:

UPGraded

My sister-in-law's Uncle Tony just died, and his tombstone is going to say:

Thanks! it was great

I feel so honored and glad to find and experience the gifts of Death each Day, and not only with Physical Death.

The Gifts Are everywhere

Here's my version of a "Death Bed"

it would be a cradle, with wings, wheels and a polka dot sail. Books, chocolate, music a phone and space for loved ones to join in and a privacy lid when not. Certain cats could visit any time.

WHAT'S GOOD WHEN PARENTS DIE

For MANY YEARS, it FELT incomprehensible TO ME THAT MY PARENTS COULD ever die. As I Grew up, I BeGAN "preGrieving" MY PARENTS DEATHS BY iMAGINING HOW it MIGHT Be WITHOUT THEM. I wondered How effective THiS kind of reHeAVSAL MIGHT Be, BUT I did it ANYWAY.

WHEN I SAW MY FATHER's deAD BODY LYING in A Bed AT A Hospice cAre center, I FeLT STUNNED BY THE reALity of it AND SAW immediAtely THAT MY reHEAVSAL HAD ALMOST NO relAtionship TO THE enormity of THiS event.

For THE 3 YEARS leAding up to MY MOTHER's deATH, I preGrieved AND reHeAVsed HEr DEATH ANYWAY, BECAUSE it FeLT Like I WAS "doing SOMETHING" in THE MidST of Feeling So HeLpless.

After MY FATHer died, MY MOTHer sAid:

> "And He's Going TO Be deAd
> SUCH A long TiMe."

I COULDN'T iMAGiNe WHAT SHe MeANT BY SAYING THAT, BUT NOW I KNOW. It's JUST AMAZING TO me THAT MY MoM is <u>still</u> deAd!

After MY pArents died, I HAVE FeLT UNBEARASLY SAD AT TiMES, AND Also resiGned, HopeLess, LOST, OrpHAned, ANGry, WistfUL, WiSHing For MOre, lonely, HeLpless, Grief STrickeN.

"Welcome to the dead parents club"

This is what my dear friend yofe shared with me after both my parents had died

recently my younger brother andrew, said to me about our mother's death:

"I wish someone had told me that it would still be sad 6 years later."

But I'll bet we wouldn't have believed it or maybe even wanted to know that. I think we all just hope it won't ever happen.

So what's good about this?

- I feel free of being witnessed or monitored, or seeing my life through their eyes

- I'm now the main storykeeper and teller in my own life. There's a certain wild freedom in that

- I feel a great sense of release now that it's over and I never need to do it again

- Our personality conflicts have ended or been transformed, and I feel closer to my parents now in some ways than when they were alive

- They can't do new dysfunctional things! some of the old patterns might still get activated, but they can't do new ones.

I've learned so many things from their successes and mistakes

- I don't need to introduce them to new people in my life, or ever attend another "guilt obligated" holiday or other occasion. I have my own rituals now and ways of doing things.

- I realize now that I'm "next in line" and my awareness of the preciousness of my life has grown significantly from experiencing their deaths

When I apply my "weaving" process to this list of things that feel good about them being dead, of course I feel an opposite for each one:

- I miss being witnessed by my mom's keen eye and great memory, and supported in my dreams and activities. I especially miss the remarkable phone conversations we used to have, and still have imaginary ones with her today

- I miss my mom's storytelling and detailed lists of who was doing what and when. She was like the family library, and it still feels shocking that that resource is gone

- Some of my fights with my father allowed me to feel connected and closer to him. I miss the possibility of arguing with him now. I miss him telling me I had mail at their house 25 years after I'd moved out

- Processing my parents' dysfunctions was one if my great interests, until I discovered all my own dysfunctions. I also miss the times they both had good things to say that contributed to my life

141

• I really miss the oppertunity to introduce new people to my parents and find it so endearing to be around friends who knew my parents "back then"

• I miss having christmas and other holidays together and am still accepting that those holidays even exist without them

i even miss the Lutheran church basement and casseroles with marshmallows only a little

• I have a deep awareness that I'm probably next in line to die, and I preferred the idea that they were there as a kind of buffer. of course it's all made up anyway, since death is mysterious and the timing of it cant be planned.

So, blending these 2 lists together leaves me in the middle, where I'm glad they're dead and sad they're dead, and everywhere in between. Sometimes it feels utterly natural that they're gone and sometimes heart-piercingly impossible.

Its all woven into that luminous material called living, and I will continue weaving, living, and witnessing others leaving, until I myself have left.

ABOUT Grief and Grieving

Grieving is not something to "Get over" as much as it is to Get into.

If we rush Grief, it just piles up in some distant place and waits to reapproach.

If we dwell too long in Grief, we color everything with it and can be consumed by it.

If we try to skip over Grief, we find it impossible.

If we try to minimize our Grieving, the unacknowledged parts reassemble and reappear later when we thought it was all finished.

If we HATE our Grief, it will maneuver for our love.

Our Grief mostly just wants our love

If we allow our Grieving, and practice sitting still or lying down and welcoming it in the slightest way, it can SHIFT, CHANGE, and Transform.

EACH Time I experience Grief, I start by trying to skip over it. NEXT I try rushing it. **Then I usually dwell** for awhile, then move straight to minimizing, and then into HATE.

When all of these fail to some degree, as they must, I surrender and finally allow

The tears, sadness, helplessness, despair, and waves of grief and grieving.

Other people try to help, of course. They say kind things, offer food or company or diversions—and these help a bit, for awhile.

Grief waits until everyone has gone home, and turns on a lamp in the corner and mutters "What about me?" And I find that grief is everywhere. Everything is a memory, or a reawakening of pain. A spoon holds a sad story. A glimpse of my mother's handwriting reminds me of her long gone, a slant of sunshine where my big black cat, now dead, used to roll in pleasure. Seemingly countless ordinary objects are growing grief memories.

Over and over, I discover and am reminded that <u>it is my resistance to grief</u> that causes it to clamor.

it is NOT grieving itself

When I can open or lean toward it, grieving can be so sweetly beautifull and I am wrapped in woven memories—of combinations of loss and gain, as well as dead and alive. It's not all <u>one</u> or the <u>other</u>. I recorded my mother's voice on a series of audiotapes before she died, and sometimes feel called to lie down with the tape recorder on my stomach and   144

Listen to her voice laughing and telling stories.

After experiencing this a few times, I became aware that I sometimes felt bored or irritated by the same things in her or her stories that had sometimes been difficult for me when she was alive. I felt amazed that I felt bored or irritated by my dead mother! Then I realized that I had the freedom to turn off the tape recorder at these times. I no longer had to listen!

and of course, I'd always had this freedom—I just didn't realize it

We all sometimes bore or irritate each other and ourselves along the way, and how we choose to handle it is part of our transformation practices.

Now when I realize that someone is boring or irritating me, it usually reflects some way that I'm not attending to myself and I decide that "they" are the problem. So often, I just need a bit of quiet or a moment alone to replenish or ground myself, or I need to speak up and ask someone for something, or I need to just leave and do something different. Our feelings are continually guiding us in grief and other emotions, and sometimes we resist their guidance. I am often resisting the guidance of my feelings! It's so easy to deny or lie, or just find my feelings inconvenient. So many times I've tried to anticipate how I'll feel when doing some activity or seeing someone, and I'll arrive feeling off center, disconnected, or crabby in some way.

Instead of just feeling what I feel, I'll often try to just "feel better." Sometimes it works and I can shift. Sometimes it doesn't work at all. Sometimes the feelings get louder or stronger and fill up my head until I can't think of anything else.

Recently on an airplane, I was seated next to someone who I found intensely annoying. His knees and elbows were in "my" space. He was eating so loudly with his mouth open—like a pig—and even turning the pages of his newspaper in a way that I found irritating.

My feelings grew so much that I knew I needed to attend to them in some way. I chose to interact with him and see what I could uncover. I commented that he must be hungry, and he replied:

"Oh, my God! I'm starving. I'm probably eating like some kind of pig. I'm so sorry. And it's really hard for me in this middle seat—I'm a big guy and I know I'm sticking out into your space too. Thank you so

146

MUCH For sitting By Me!"

I FELT an immediate rush of love Fr Him.

I immediately relaxed and FELT So GlAd THAT I HAd spoken up, and tended to My FeeliNGs too.

He and I ended up playing cards and lAUGHiNG Until The woman BeHind Us Asked Us if we could pleAse Be A little Quieter. I knew just How she FeLt, and we lowered our volume.

Our FeeliNGs will respond Quickly To our CAre and Attention, and wHen we stay tuned in during Grieving or oTHer kinds of Feelings, We will FeeL GlAd A lot More of The Time.

FEELINGS DIAL

stay tuned in . . .

WHAT TO SAY TO A GRIEVING PERSON

We forget that our love matters, that our presence counts and comforts. This awareness is more important than what we actually say. The words don't matter as much as our tone or intention.

A grieving person is generally seeking: comfort, acknowledgment, honoring, recognition, validation, inspiration, connection. Gestures matter.

I still remember a bouquet of flowers I received from my friend Val and her mom after my mom died. Multi-colored Gerbera Daisies in a low glass bowl arrived on a chilly fall day in Minnesota, and those flowers were with me during one of the loneliest weeks of my life.

People sometimes feel scared that nothing they can do for the grieving person is "enough." And in a way, it's true. Nothing is enough, because it can't erase pain or bring someone or something back. But it can soothe, remind, and surround with a profound feeling of support.

Being remembered at times of grief or loss has a potent effect. I still have the cards, notes, letters and printouts of emails I received after my DAD, MOM, and CAT died.

THe worlds THAT people SHAred were
SOUL rAiSiNG

for me.

Sometimes people feel overwHeLMed By Grief of THeir own and simply cant reAcH out. rememBer THis if you dont HeAr From someone you THoUGHT you Would HeAr From.

don't BLAMe THem
or Yourself, if you cant reach out

After someone HAS died, dont stop sAyiNG THAT Person's NAMe or THink THAT THe Grieving person doesnt Wаnt To HeAr it.

I Still FeeL Moved wHen someone sAys my Mom's NAMe, and sHe's Been deAd More THAN 6 yeArs.

It can Be tempting To THink THAT THe Grieving person will Be sAdder if you Bring up THeir loss. THis is unlikely, and even if it occurs, THe e-Motions Are MoviNG, and THis is Good.

Grief is loNG-lAstiNG, and if you're not Able To reAcH out riGHT AwAy, THere will Be oTHer Opportunities To sHAre love wiTH A Grieving person.

It is never too lAte
To offer love or comforT

THINGS TO SAY TO A GRIEVING PERSON

* you can also utilize the quotes in this book

○ Bless you and the spirit of _____. I am here and available for you

○ I've lit a little lamp in my heart for you at this time

○ There are no words to speak, only my love to share

○ I just love you so much — at this time especially

○ **Know that our hearts are full of love** right now for you

○ As you grieve, I am reminding you that I can be there in a moment, in person or by phone or email. I'll check in with you too

○ remember that you are all ways surrounded by love, I love you so much

○ Just honoring and acknowledging your pain and loss, and all of your feelings

Speak about death, loss, change, and grief. express your emotions with your words, in your particular way and style. Your unique expression, even if it seems ordinary to you, will be so appreciated.

THINGS NOT TO SAY TO A GRIEVING PERSON

○ NO THING

○ It's FOR THE BEST, BECAUSE THEY'RE not
   SuffERING anymore *
   * SAY THIS only if THEY SAY it first

○ How old were They? AFTER ALL, THEY HAD A
   long Life *
   * THE GriEViNG person often Wauts it to Be longer

○ I KNOW How you FEEL. Our DOG died THis
   YEAr, and it's ROUGH *
   * you don't KNOW How They FEEL, and it's _not_ THE SAME

○ Let us Know if THERE's anyThing we can do *
   * Well MeaniNG, But FAlls short of any ACTuAL
     Gesture or HELP — an outdATed, HABituAted response —
     Also Means They need to contAct you

if you HAVE MATERIAL GiFTS To offer, send or BRiNG THeM.
Do not rely on THE GrieVING person to CAll you and ASK.
     I still remember THe deep KiNDNESS of My
friend JAN, WHO WOULD CAll and SAY TO me WHEN I
Arrived TO visit My dying Mom in MinnesotA:

   "Here's THe fun and inspiring THings we can
     do TOGeTHer while you're Here."
     And sHE would Give me A list — and I was temporarily
Lifted out of THE MiASMA of sADness I WAS LiviNG in.
GrieVing is A part of All of our Lives — and not only
WHEN people die. We GrieVe our losses, WHETHer we
ACKNOWLedGe it or Not. GrieVe As you BreATHe — consisteutly.   151

DEATH or LOSS of ANIMALS

I THINK THAT every Beloved animal is so precious and unusual in their ordinary animal ways. THey Are Certainly our primary unconditional love teachers, and BECAUSE of THeir shorter Life spans, THey TEACH us profound lessons ABout loss and CHange.

I lived WITH and loved A BiG BLACK CAT NAMed Jupiter for 17 years and over Time, GRADUALly BECAME one of THe "CAT oBsessed" people I HAD misunderstood and MOCKed in THe BeGinning.

Mostly, Jupiter GAve me My first significant experiences of animal love since My CHILDHOOD dog NAMed PUNKY. I leArned so MUCH ABout loss WHen Jupiter died. He continues To Be an unconditional love mentor To me To This DAy.

Here Are JUST A Few of Jupiter's GIFTS:
He "discovered" My "How To Be an ARTIST" poster,
WHICH HUNG on THE WALL of My MAGIC cottAGe, By
STanDinG on His HinD LEGS and CLAWinG it off THe WALL,
WHere it WOULD land WITH A

W
H
o
o
S
H !

And wAke me up. After A week of THIS, I finally
"Listened" to WHAT Jupiter WAS COMMUNICATING, and took it
TO A STore THAT HAd A CATALOG and Asked if THey'd
Like to PUBLISH it.
            THey SAid "it's crooked and odd, But we'll see—don't expect MUCH"

I ended up creatinG over 11,000 posters By Hand,
and THen releAsinG it TO Be printed, WHere it SOLD 2
Million copies.

    Jupiter "kept WATCH" WHile I creATed My
fiVST puBLisHed BOOK, A creAtive Companion, WHICH
is in its 13ᵗʰ printinG toDAy.

    AS I reAd More ABOUT THE possibility/proBABility
of A lArGe eArTHQUAKe in THE BAY AreA, I TAUGHT
Jupiter To DiG me out of rUBBLe By coverinG
Myself WITH oBJects and THen callinG for His HELP.
He WOULD DiG and DiG until He HAd completely
unCovered me, MeowinG THE WHOLE TiMe.

Since I'd decided to let Jupiter be an indoor and outdoor cat, it felt scary to let him out at night, since there were lots of raccoons in the neighborhood and they were known to attack cats. One night, I heard a terrible screaming sound coming from my garden, only to look out the window to see Jupiter riding around in circles on the back of a raccoon!

I never worried again

Most of all, Jupiter was with me each day and night as I lived my life. He began sleeping with me, finding a spot on my pillow for his big black head. Each day, he would awaken me by licking my third eye until I started laughing.

I sang to him, told him stories, and learned to communicate with him in animal language from one of the premier people in this field, Penelope Smith.

I shared my fears, anxieties, and nightmares with Jupiter, as well as my joys, triumphs, successes, and dreams.

His energy was so Buddha-like, people loved to house-sit, take care of Jupiter, and "consult" with him while I traveled. I learned to take care of another creature as I learned to take care of myself, and I literally thought that if he ever died, I would die, too.

154

My Brother Andrew had concerns about my level of devotion and care, and periodically warned me that Jupiter was an animal and would likely die before me.

i knew this logically, but emotionally I'd decided that Jupiter simply couldn't die

I felt sure that Jupiter would be the oldest cat who ever lived, and I took care of him with Acupuncture, raw foods, energy medicine, and daily massages.

About a year after my Mom died, Jupiter got really sick and started collapsing when he tried to walk. For the next nine months, I took him to see the best vets, fed him extra-nourishing food, and took such exquisite care of him as he began to get worse. He'd developed kidney disease and a few other conditions, and I learned to give him fluids daily with a needle so he wouldn't get dehydrated or be in more pain. My Brother helped me, Friends were so supportive, and I Also hired a wonderfull woman to come in and administer other medications and treatments when I needed to go to work.

My home turned into a Hospice care center as I prayed for him to "Get well" but knew he was dying.

155

I started going on longer walks each day to deal with my grief and prepare for the coming loss. One night, he went behind the couch where he had never gone, and I felt certain that he'd crawled back there to die. I felt so completely and utterly exhausted, I decided that if he died I couldn't bear to know that night and that he'd still be dead in the morning, and I went to bed.

I awakened at 3 a.m. to him licking my third eye— he was still alive and loving me! it was such a miracle

A few days later, as I watched him struggle to breathe or even sit up, I knew it was time to assist him in dying. I called my closest friends, my brother, and the woman I'd hired who had provided such tender care— I knew that everyone there loved him. I also called a mobile vet who arrived like a true angel to help me, and to help Jupiter to die.

By the light of dozens of candles, in my little cottage, I held Jupiter in my arms as the vet gave the injection. In that instant, I saw Jupiter's spirit fly straight up, and

I FELT THAT His BODY WAS releAsed. His fur
Svddenly AppeNred SOFT and stiny and I Asked
everyone to leave so I could JUST sit with His
still WArM CAT BODY.

After Awhile, I reAlized THAT He WAS
Getting COLD and stiff, and THAT it WAS TiMe
for me to Get up. Jupiter's BODY WAS now
So stiff, it Appeared to Be Like A BiG BLACK
purse, and I stArted Hysterically LAUGHING
AS I Fit Him into His kitty cArrier to Be
creMATed The next DAy.

I THen went WALKING AT My FAVorite
BeAcH and HAD Mystical experiences with
STArFisH, seALS, and A tiny BLAck
puppy NAMed . . . . Jupiter.

yes, really

I WAS Actually publicizing A new Book
During This Time, and THere WAS A BOOK
event ALreAdy scheduled in Advance for
THAT night. of course, no one expected me
to Go, After Jupiter Dying THAT Afternoon.
I consulted with My Guides and Jupiter's spirit
and went To speak THAT night After All.
I spoke About Jupiter and lArge, seemingly
insurMountAble Grief and BiG LOVE.

157

The next night, I had a dream where Jupiter was a human-sized cat, and was slow dancing with me. When I woke up, I could still feel his paw in the small of my back.

About a year later, I was presenting at one of my favorite conferences called Celebrate your Life and saw a friend and shaman I often work with in the spiritual and health realms. He said:

"Oh, my Goodness. Jupiter has turned into a spirit guide! He's standing right behind you, about a head taller than you, and he's wearing purple. Can you feel him?"

I said that I could and smiled at how good it felt.

About an hour later, I was being interviewed for a TV show with James Van Praagh, who among many other gifts, communicates with dead people and spirits—and who is a friend of mine. As soon as he saw me, he said,

"Honey—you've got yourself a big old spirit guide. He's a big black cat, taller than you, standing behind you and wearing purple!"

I smiled again, and continue to feel Jupiter in various spiritual forms.

158

As I write This, it's The 6th anniversary of His physical DeATH, and I couldn't HAve imagined How much richer, BrighTer, and deeply self-loving My Life could Be wiThouT Him.

A Friend's FATHer visited and rATHer insensitively Asked me, "HAve you replaced THAT CAT yet?" I angrily said no and How He could ASK THAT. Would He ASK if I HAd replaced My MoTHer?

People say All kinds of odd Things

The Following yeAr The SAme Friend's FATHer visited and Asked me The SAme Question. This Time I HAd Figured it out.

He wAs reAlly JusT Asking me if I HAd enough Love in My Life

I Assured Him THAT I HAd enough love and THanked Him For inQuiring. BecAuse The unconditionAl love lessons HAd Been infused into me. Jupiter HAd so purely reflected unconditionAl love THAT it HAd chAnged My very cells. I know THAT AnimALs can do This. They Are profound TeAchers, and I

159

AM SO GLAD and GRATEFULL TO HAVE LIVED WITH and loved one of THE very BEST.

Before Jupiter died, HE ASKED TO BE an oracle on my WEBSite and SAID THAT He HAD information To SHARE. SO I copied down WHAT He TOLD ME, and we FED it into THE computer and created A PLACE WITH drawings and photos of HiM called "ASK Jupiter." He's Kind of Like an enLightened MAGiC 8 BAll— UNcanny in His ACCUrACy. planetSARK.com.

He Also toLD me Before He died: "We animals don't MiND DyiNG AT All. It's Like UNzipping our Fur and stepping out of it to do SOMETHiNG else. You reAlly don't need To Be SAd, UNless you WANT TO."
                  and I Believe HiM

ABout 5 yeArs AFter Jupiter died, while I WAS writing THe FirST DrAFT of THis BOOK, one of MY neiGHBors cleaned some THinGS out of A STOrAGe AreA we All SHAred. I HAD cAreFully HiDDen THis roCK some Kind SOUL HAD Given Me WiTH Jupiter's NAMe and yeAr of DeATH cArved into it, BecAuSe I WASn't reAdy TO see it or HAve it Around. On THe dAy I WAS STArTiNG To write ABout Jupiter, THere it WAS, on A ledGe outside My coTTAGe. JuPiter WAS letting Me KNow THAT I WAS reAdy.

160

"I HAVE found THE pArAdox
THAT if you love until it HurTs,
THere can be no more Hurt,
only more love"   MoTHer TeresA

screen   of   contemplation

@ Be fiercely ALive

@ Do THis by expanding your AWAreness
of THis moment

@ reveL in THe wonders of Life and
anticipate deATH As A GreAT Adventure

◀   ⬡ || ▶

Qvotes   For   cHANGe

"I HAVe only slipped AwAy into THe next room,
I Am I and you Are you, wHATever we were to eAcH
oTHer, THAT we Are still. CALL me By My OLD FAmiliAr
NAme. speAk To me in THe eAsy wAY wHicH you
AlwAys used. PLAY, smile, THink of me. All is well"

162

"I'm not going to die.
I'm going Home Like A
SHooTing STAr"
Sojourner TruTH

BOOKS

- HeALing Grief JAmes Van prAAGH
- The crAGGy Hole in my HeArt and
  The cAt who Fixed it GeneeA roTh
- Grieving THe DEATH of A PeT Betty J. CArmAck
- THe Grace in Dying KATHleen Dowling Singh
- Being present in The DArkness CHeri Huber
- LiGHTs in Blue sHadows edie HartsHorne
- THe Kingdom of HeArt PATTy L. LuckenBACH, M.A., D.D.
- THe Power of Now eCKHArt Tolle
- UnFinisHed Business JAmes Van prAAGH
- HeArtBroken open Kristine CArlson

weB resources

- CAringbridge.com
- Life-preservers.org
- LiGHTning-strike.com
- LivingcompAssion.com
- HeALingenvironments.org
- JAkesAKe.com
- BeliefneT.com
- TUT.com
- sexysoulwellness.com
- LeArningToForgive.com

Music

sACred om
NAdine risHA.com

" I HAVE Always looked upon decAY
As being just As wonderful and
rich an expression As GrowTH "
Henry Miller

Transformation
Practices

LEARNING TO TRANSFORM LOSSES INTO GIFTS

While writing about loss for this book, I felt as sad as dirt. This happens sometimes. Even thinking about loss can bring more feelings of loss forward. I call it "loss multiplying." It's where one loss reminds you of another, and another and it can multiply and become MORE than it even is.

There are ways to focus on these thoughts for transformational purposes without becoming consumed by them. We all have kind of an "ambient loss awareness" that operates behind the scenes in our consciousness. It is often untended consciously by us, which can result in "loss multiplying." New experiences of loss can then stack up on previously unconscious or untended ones, and we can feel pretty awful— even more awful than what we've lost, or are afraid of losing! Before I had done my transformational work about my dad traveling so much in my childhood, anytime anyone current in my life left, it would multiply the original loss.

Practicing feeling our losses, and then transforming them into gifts and opportunities too, provides a more spacious perspective to live with. For example, my dad had a lot of anger issues, and his being gone a lot spared me from living with them. Integrating our losses like this sets us free to truly feel "glad no matter what happens."

165

Creating your own Loss List

The purpose of This loss List is to experience and express your emotions about The loss and Grief That Live in The Background of your Life, So That you can experience The Gifts and Opportunities That Live within each loss and practice Transforming each one. It does not Take a long Time to Feel. It Takes a lot longer To resist Feeling.

Here's one of my loss Lists:

1. Loss of relationship with older Brother
2. Loss and change of my previous physical Mobility
3. Loss of Mom and Dad and idealizations of Them
4. Loss of my Cat and physical experiences of unconditional love
5. Loss of youth and a certain kind of "Attractiveness"
6. Loss of a Joy-full loving Childhood - The idealized version
7. Loss of ever Feeling "normal"
8. Loss of ever Being a Birth Mom
9. Loss of significant Friendships
10. Loss and change of particular Dreams
11. Loss of Taking Good Health For Granted
12. Loss of Family members Due to unhealthy Dynamics

I recommend spending some Time just feeling SAD or whatever other feelings Arise After creating a List like This. This is a necessary and Helpful part of your Transformation and change process.

Allow Tears To Flow

FEEL SO SAD

Cry me A river

Practicing Transformation and Change

Take your loss List and Ask yourself The following Questions:

- How have I experienced each loss?

- What Transformations and Changes have Taken place?

- What Gifts and opportunities Lie within each Loss, and How can I Transform and Change Further?

We'll practice exploring with Some of my loss List, Then you can practice with Some of your own.

- I learned From losing my relationship with my older Brother That I Deeply love Him, even Though He Sexually and Physically Abused me As A Child, and is A Practicing Drug Addict and Alcoholic As An Adult. I have The opportunity to Practice Forgiving Him and The man who Abused Him. The main Gift That resulted From This relationship is my Awareness, and His Beautifull Daughter—my niece and Goddaughter. I've changed my previous Judgments About Addictions and Am telepathically Transforming my previous relationship with my older Brother into A new one That contains only love.

① My experiences of chronic pain from a dance injury affected my ability to walk without pain. I had the opportunity to practice patience and humility. The main gift is that now I treasure dancing and walking pain-free. I changed my physical exercise program and learned a new system of self-care called positional release that allows me to put my muscles into alignment. I am also transforming my relationship with my body into one with even more acceptance and self-care.

② Now that my parents are both dead, I have the opportunity to integrate the gifts of their deaths into my life. The main gifts are that they existed and gave life to me, and that I love them. Their spiritual energy shelters me. I've changed my harsh judgments about how they parented me and feel glad for all the joy we experienced together. I've transformed all my residual anger and fear about my parents into pure love.

Now, I'd like you to practice this process with one or more of your losses. Find the opportunities, gifts, changes and transformations. This will literally change the cells of your body and allow you to experience a whole new way of living with loss and changes. 169

Loss or Change Transformation Sheet

I feel loss about:

What transformations or changes have taken place, and/or what am I planning?

Are there gifts and opportunities within this loss? What are they?

What is my new story or perspective about this loss or change?

Telling and Living New Stories

Grief, loss and change can result in our living in old stories. We repeat the stories to try to understand the pain. We sometimes get stuck there. Stories get repeated so often, they become like ruts in the road.

We sigh. We say we're sad. We describe "What Happened." Someone listens.

Of course this is all very important and necessary. It just often goes on much longer than the feelings even do. Then each time we retell it, the feelings are reawakened and we think we're still "there."

Meanwhile, we and our feelings have moved on, and we forget or don't know how to change our stories.

For years I told the stories of my older brother abusing me and how much it scared and hurt me.

Incest stories are very important to tell AND at a certain point the retelling and sympathetic responses can be counterproductive

Years later, I discovered that my brother had been abused by a neighbor and hadn't just turned into what felt like a monster overnight.

My stories started to change to include understanding, compassion, and forgiveness for my brother and myself, and also our great friendship and love that had existed earlier when he was my "Big Brother," showing me how to catch snapping turtles in the creek near our house.

My previous stories only highlighted the abuse part, and the more I repeated them, the more iconic they became. The stories, in fact, identified me as a "survivor." Certainly survival is important— very important— but at some point surviving wasn't enough. I felt ready to complete my surviving journey and start thriving and just living. The old stories didn't support either, so I told them less and less, or told them differently.

I started telling new stories, about how my brother had a daughter and I love her so much. That the neighbor who had abused had surely been abused himself. I learned that many girls in the neighborhood had been abused, how it wasn't "just me."

Then I started living more in the feeling state of the new stories. This involved meditation, physical rituals and repeating stories of empowerment and grace.

It isn't THAT I forgot or condoned WHAT HAPPENED TO ME; I just stopped telling THE story THAT WAY.

I forgave my brother.

I forgave my parents.

I'm still forgiving THE THERAPIST who let me sit on his lap when I was 7, and then I heard him say through the door: "You have a very seductive little girl and I think that the problems in this family are because of her." THAT'S WHAT I THOUGHT I HEARD

I now envision THE THERAPIST also possibly saying: "WHAT A wonderful child your DAUGHTER is! There are some mysteries to solve in your FAMILY, but you have lovely, lively children, and I promise to help your family to feel better."

I don't actually know which story is "true," but the body doesn't care, and my spirit and emotions are practicing living and telling new stories!

I started asking friends if I was repeating stories, and if so, which ones. I questioned myself to see if I still needed those stories. In each case, I didn't.

Now I question my stories. I go underneath them to see what's there.

If there are lingering stories that I tell with myself as any kind of victim, I take the story apart until I can tell it in a completely neutral way with no "charge" against something or someone else.

and of course this is an art and a practice, so it's often imperfect

Living this way has resulted in tremendous freedom

It's also cleared the way for new stories and experiences.

THANK GOODNESS

I TAKE 100% responsibility for everything THAT HAppens—even if I Think THAT someone else HAS done something Awful or Hurtful

of course, I'm not Always "successful" in These practices. THAT'S WHY I practice, so it can Become My first response instead of My second or Third. **It's often My first response now.**

I used To Think it WAS Helpful to listen to others' stories endlessly—to BEAr witness As long AS They needed to tell THem. **NOW I SPEAK up and SAY WHAT I see.** Sometimes Gently, sometimes Not.

i usually Ask for permission

If someone isn't TAKing responsibility or MAKing CHanGes, I lose Interest in listening and now realize it's Actually HARMful not to speak up — Because The story energy Gets stronger The More it's told, and Then its More difficult To CHanGe.

I do The SAMe WITH Myself and Check in WITH close Friends to see if They Are Able to Hear me—or Not. If I'm still in A pAttern of needing To retell A certAin story, I'll find A Friend WHo HAS The CApAcity to listen,

175

OR write my own story down and explore it until I can feel it changing.

I had a profound physical experience of this recently when I went BOWLING and knocked down all the pins except a couple. My old story was that on my next ball, I would never get the pins left over. I used to get really nervous when I saw all the space around those pins, and I would "stutter step" up to the point of throwing the ball, and almost never get those pins knocked down.

I reinforced this story by retelling and then re-experiencing it.

One day while bowling, I said to myself: "I'm done with this old story. I focus on the pins and not on the space around them."

I stepped up to bowl and became a spare pin bowling machine, knocking down nearly every one! I felt astonished to see how the living of my new story so dramatically changed the physical results. I'm practicing this with all my stories now, and consequently am living more joy-fully "in the moment" than I ever have.

I created this quote to support me and others.

"The opposite of old is not young.
The opposite of old is new.
As long as we continue to experience
the new, we will gloriously
inhabit all of the ages that we are."

let's do more of the new more often

Living in The Middle
A process for weaving a new way of living

I've long been prone to extremes and dramatic declarations—especially during times of loss or change.

After my love relationship ended, I experienced relentless sad feelings where I was missing her and "us" so much, I didn't see how I could continue feeling those sad feelings.

During one particularly sad time, I decided to make a list of everything I missed about her— from the tiny to the large. There were hundreds of items.

I just sat there crying and reading it.

Then I had the idea to see how many opposites I could find— things I didn't miss. I went through the whole list if hundreds and found an opposite for each one!

This Amazed me

After creating and reading these 2 lists, I had this profound experience of living in the middle — neither missing her or not missing her.

It felt solid and blended and very real to be in this middle place.

I felt like I could access unconditional loving from the middle place, instead of either idealizing or demonizing her and our past relationship.

I've realized that suffering comes from comparing

How it WAS
To
How it is NOW

I'm utilizing this weaving process to break free from what I'm calling the "polarized spell" where everything is extreme, either/or, Good/Bad, idealized or demonized.

I remember various therapists and mentors pointing out that I had a very "black and white" view, and that I could benefit from more of a "Gray Area" I never liked

The idea of an Area Being gray, so I didnt really explore more ABOUT THis idea.

Now I see THAT THe Middle is such A rich, expansive place. I WAS living in THe MArgins of THe extremes.

and it's not gray At All!

Perhaps "Middle Age" is just another way of saying

Living in THe Middle

I THink so

So Now I'M using Lists of opposites for All THe subjects in My Life— WHAT I love/HATe, do/don't ABout any given subject. In eACH cAse, upon completion of BoTH Lists, I find Myself propelled into THe Middle— WiTH A MuCH wider, More forgiving perspective.

Here's an example if one of my lists:

SUBJECT: To get 1 or 2 kittens or not

Do
1. More love
2. Adorableness
3. Tiny Heart Beats
4. Curled up Together
5. Unconditional love

Don't
1. less Freedom
2. Care and feeding
3. Vet Bills
4. Care while I'm Away
5. memories of unconditional love loss

The Middle

Where it's great and okay and annoying and ordinary — To get Them or not and its all the same

My notes:

One day, I'll probably get 2 kittens. Right now, I'm enjoying my Freedom and time of not caring for other living Beings. The years of caring for my dying mother and dying cat gave me the gifts of not needing to care for them. Ultimately... it's all the same — getting cats or not. There will always be love from all the inexhaustible sources, and I'm just living in the "Marvelous middle" where it all mixes together.

Here's a Template of a List so you
can create your own:

Subject:

Do: Don't:

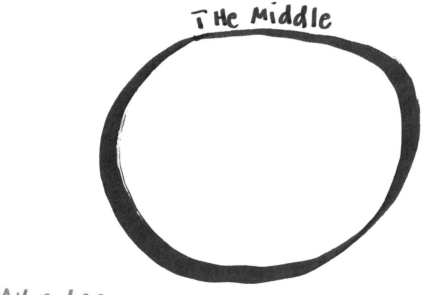

The Middle

My notes:

I think that we naturally want to
live in the middle and are conditioned to
live in the extremes— and then habitually
remain there.

Some of the greatest idealizing occurs
when someone dies. Often we only remember
what was good...

which is blatantly untrue and unfair
to the dead person

This type of idealizing also serves to
capture people in grief long after they've
actually completed a grieving period.

Allowing the middle way would
provide great relief

We often demonize someone when they
do something wrong, and then <u>freeze</u> them
there, keeping the pain in place.

Allowing the middle way would provide
movement and release.

Now I'm on the lookout for words
that signify the "extremes:"

never. Always. worst. Best

I'm actively practicing my weaving
process to be in the middle as often as I can.

My 6 year-old godchild, Jonah, told me about some of his adventures at Disneyland recently, and I asked him to tell me what he loved. He talked excitedly about so many things and then said:

"Susan, want to know what I HATED?"

I replied eagerly that I did, and he leaned over and whispered:

"Not many people realize this, but the Matterhorn has a Monster. It's not just a good place."

I loved seeing his natural weaving of the Middle Place

TODAY at the grocery store, I let a woman go in front of me in line, and we discussed our work lives briefly. When she discovered that I worked at home, she exclaimed:

"THAT would be just the BEST"

I gently pointed out that this is a common idealization—that people forget or don't know about the downsides to it. She started laughing and said:

"Good point!"

I replied:

"I THINK WE ALL THINK THERE'S
ALWAYS SOMETHING GREAT THAT
WE DON'T HAVE!"

THEN WE STARTED TALKING ABOUT THINGS
THAT WE COMMONLY DEMONIZE, AND WE BOTH
WALKED AWAY WITH NEW PERSPECTIVES.

WEAVING A WAY TO LIVE IN THE MIDDLE
IS A MORE EXPANSIVE, GLAD WAY TO
PRACTICE LIVING.

I LIKE TO REMIND PEOPLE OF THIS
MIDDLE WAY BY SAYING:

"ON A DARKER NOTE...."
INSTEAD OF "ON A LIGHTER NOTE" BECAUSE
WE ONLY EVER HEAR THE SECOND ONE.

LOSS or CHANGE of DREAMS

DREAMS do not GET LOST. They will WAIT forever and Are very resilient. I experienced This directly when my Biggest dreAM AT 10 YEArs OLD, of Being "A BEACON of Hope and writing BOOKS for THE world," didn't physically Manifest until 25 yeAvs lATer AT Age 35, After Years of self-destructive BeHavior and wild Living.

. Every Morsel of everything I experienced in THose yeArs Between 10 and 35 HAS Been, or is BeiNG, Utilized By my dreAMS toDAy. NoTHing was LOST, WASted, or Broken in THe process, even THoughH THe inner critics will tell you it WAS. inner critics Ne not riGHT! Don't listen TO THem. Give THem new JoBs to do.

I've ALso Been WOrKing with people and THeir crertive dreAMS for Over 20 yeNs now, and Can tell you THAT we Ne All full and BursTing WITH creAtive dreAMS — even if we don't Know eXActly WHAT THey Are! CreAtive DreAMs HAVE A Life force and energy of THeir own THAT will find wAys To Be MAde visiale.

DreAMs can and do CHanGe sHAye. I HAD dreAMs of riding A CAMeL Across AFRica After I reAd **TRACKS** By roByn DAvidson. THAT DreAM 186

HAS CHANGED into TRAVELING to AFRICA or finDING A BABY CAMEL to Adopt.

Dreams do not Always Get smaller either— I HAD A Dream of BUYING My MAGIC COTTAGE and BOUGHT THAT and THE BUILDING BEHIND it. I Dreamed of MAKING "products to inspire Creative Living" and created A Lifestyle Brand called SARK.

I consistently witness and Assist people in "WAKING up" To THeir long-HELD Creative dreams and **doing** THEM. Many people utilize My MicroMovement process, WHICH I will describe in THIS Book. It's A GreAT WAY To Keep Dreams consistently and Gladly Moving.

Dreams love to Move, To Be seen and HeArd, and To Become ReAL.

THAT's WHere you come in.

We MAKe dreams real primarily Because we're DeLIGHTed in some WAY.

- deLIGHT drives desire
- desire and PRACTICAL Gladness MAKe Creative dreams

ReAL

Micromovement Wheels of Delight

Many years ago, I invented a method for myself called Micromovements.

It's a simple way to start and keep going. I like to use wheels in this process because they represent motion.

Micromovements are like ignition devices. They're 5 sec—5 min in length, because I figured out that I could do just about anything for 5 minutes, and you probably can too.

60% of the time, once you do a Micromovement, you will <u>keep going</u>—most times for many hours

40% of the time, you'll stop after 5 minutes, and this is wonderfull too, because the brain doesn't care whether you did 5 minutes or 5 hours on your dream. It just knows that <u>something is happening</u>.

Micromovements lead to huge results and cause substantial growth. I use them to create all my books and help me operate my life.

And the Micromovement wheels keep all the projects separate, in their own "homes" and out of your head! Many people use their brains as filing cabinets, and they can get very crowded as years go by!

Let's play Micromovement wheels! 188

MicroMovement Wheels of Delight

We do things much more easily when we're delighted
Tiny movements of 5 sec – 5 min add up to HUGE results. It's like an ignition system

Here's a self-care self-love example

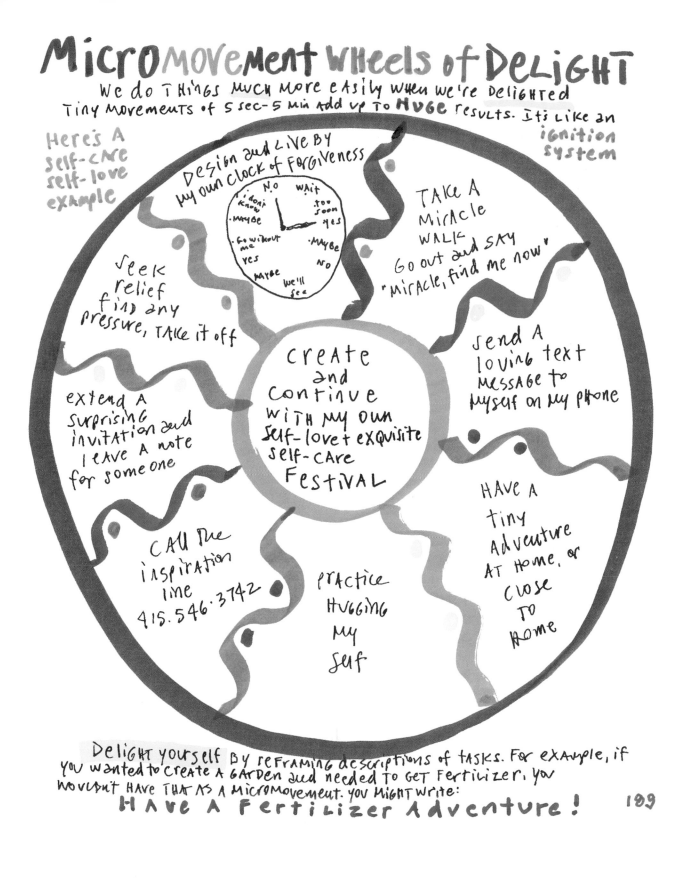

Design and live by my own clock of Forgiveness

NO   WAIT
·i don't know   ·too soon
·MAYBE   yes
·Go without   ·MAYBE
me yes   NO
MAYBE   we'll see

TAKE A MiRACLE WALK
Go out and SAY "MiRACLE, find me now"

Seek relief find any pressure, TAKE it off

Send A loving text message to myself on my phone

extend A surprising invitation and I leave A note for someone

CREATE and continue WITH MY own Self-love + exquisite self-care Festival

HAVE A tiny Adventure AT Home, or close to Home

CALL the inspiration line 415.546.3742

practice hugging my self

Delight yourself by reframing descriptions of tasks. For example, if you wanted to create a garden and needed to get fertilizer, you wouldn't have that as a micromovement. You might write:

HAVE A Fertilizer Adventure!

189

You can make Micromovement wheels for All the subjects in your Life, and with just a little practice, you can make paying your taxes as delight-full as planning a vacation! It Also keeps All your projects moving even when you're not working on them. It Also creates a habit of completion and Allows more Joy in your Life!

Use them For All sorts of subjects and projects: decluttering, healthcare, creative dreams, writing, revisioning your Life

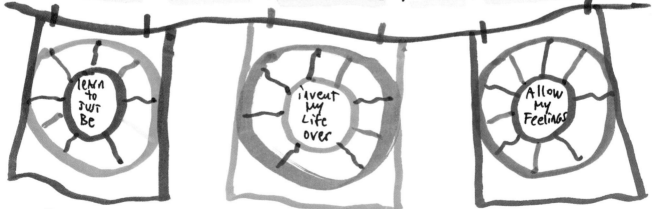

This system is customizable for you. If wheels don't appeal, use scraps of paper, index cards, post-its — anything that delights you. You'll love making inspired movements to do more of what you love.

MicroMovement Wheel of Delight

To inspire you

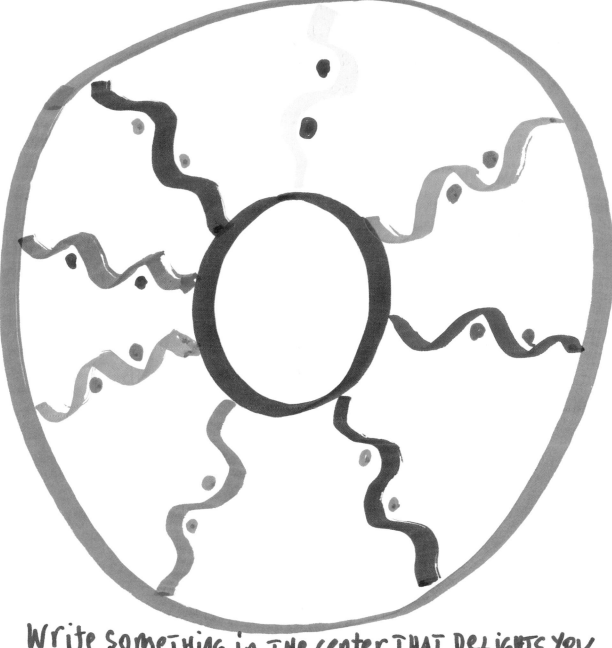

Write something in the center that delights you that you want to make real. Then, choose Micromovements.

MirAcle WALKS WITH SARK

One of my greATesT gladnesses is going on WHAT I call "MirAcle WALKS."

THis is wHere you Go out wiTH no AgendA or destinATion and say out loud or to yourself:

"Miracles, find me now!"

YesterdAy I weut To My FAvorite BeACH To TAKe A WALK and Asked For A MirAcle to find me. THis Time I used THe words:

"SHOW me MirAculous People."

I Arrived AT THe WArMing HuT, A MArvelous stATe PArK CAfe riGHT neAr THe Golpen GATe Bridge, and ordered my FAvorite sandwicH. As I WAited, I noticed THAT All THe TABles were full, except For one spot in Between lots of people, so I wedged in THere.

THe two people sitting next To me — A WOMAn wiTH spArKly eyes and A young MAn of some succulence — were exHibiting A certAin luminous energy. So I Asked THe WoMan ABout Her soup, and sHe said it WAs delicious toMAto BAsil and THAt sHe would Be HAPPy to sHAre. I said THAt I'd be HAPPy to sHAre 1/2 my sandwicH too.

So we HAppily sHAred.

The young man asked me how I was, who I was, and I leaned forward and answered:

"I am just so madly in love with myself!"

They both laughed heartily and deeply and shared that they had just been at Grace Cathedral, hearing about "finding the miracles in every moment" and that clearly this was one!

And so I had met my first miraculous people: Ann and her son Dodd from New Orleans and New York.

Two women at the next table were happily eavesdropping and asked me about the miracle moments and about me loving myself.

We all began talking together and I discovered two more miraculous people: Alissa and Marianne, who run a non profit and were at the warming hut solving a business challenge. We all started discussing resources and serendipities.

I shared that I was SARK, who they knew, and as it turns out, Marianne lives in my neighborhood in San Francisco! Marianne then had a vision about Dodd, who is involved in new york theatre, and Marianne had a fabulous resource for him. I then had a vision about Dodd, and asked if he knew about parallel universes, and that we're all living in them, All Different Times in History stacked up next to each other. He did know About them and said that his off-Broadway play called LUCK has a section in the middle About parallel universes!

I Actually saw 3 versions of Dodd Through History As he sat There— different Ages, Different Clothes, same person. Dodd Then realized that He Also knew SARK. He had gone to HAWAii with A previous girlfriend trying to get A job At A Noni FARM. While clutching the SARK book Succulent Wild Woman, his girlfriend had told him That They must Apply for the position using the word "succulent."

They did get Accepted At The Noni FARM

I told Dodd That he was A succulent wild man, and that Dodd is A "succulent Ass Name."

His mom especially Liked This

By This point, other people At other tables started joining our conversation, including Authors, Artists and one very loud poet.

Marianne and Alissa and I walked down the Beach And continued our serendipitous conversation, Marveling At the results of our respective "Miracle WALKS" and Miraculous people.

194

Recently while creating this book, I got sick and while recovering, could only go on a tiny miracle walk — just a few hundred yards — close to my home. I stood on my front step and said:

"Miracle, find me now."

And my next-door neighbor materialized, out walking her dog. I've known her for about 20 years but had never been inside her home. A few years ago, she completed a 2 year total renovation of her building and invited me to see it, and it just never happened.

So she invited me this night, and I went in. I swear I heard angelic music playing as I looked up the curving wooden steps — like a snail shell leading up to her gorgeous loft-like living space. I immediately noticed that her kitchen table was the same as the one from my childhood, and that her cupboards contained the plastic horses I used to play with!

She let me take them out, and I played and marveled that these toys from the '50's were in her home. I began to feel like I was in some kind of movie as she showed me around, and I saw her gleamingly beautifull closet full of what appeared to be costumes.

195

I SAW A HUGE computer screen and Blurted out:

"WHAT do you do for a Living?"

She smiled and replied THAT she designs Barbie doll clothes.

I WAS JUST Glowing AT The idea of This creative woman Living and working right next door to me All These years and wondering, if We Lifted off All The rooftops, How many other Miracles we would see and know about too.

We're All Miracles, Here in Human form

remember to ask for Miracles to Appear, and Then practice recognizing Them when They do. They Are sometimes disguised As something unattractive or even ugly. Adjust your vision, and request more information.

Incorporate Miracles and Miracle walks into your Life, and I promise THAT you'll Be More deLighted, and Able To More easily DELIGHT OThers.

Awareness Practices for Miracle Walking and Miracle Spotting

@ Putting your Hands out and Asking for a Miracle is powerfull all by itself and will draw Miracles to you. The other day I saw something crumpled in the crook if a Tree and found a $10 bill!

This proves that money grows on trees

@ Training yourself to see Miracles everywhere — At the Mall, the DMV, the grocery store — anywhere people gather. I went to my car dealership to Have them check the tire Because I had an intuition that something Was wrong. They found a nail, and while it was being repaired, I complimented the people who worked there and because of this, they discounted the bill by 50%

@ Allowing Miracles to come from "ordinary situations". While I was seated at a cafe last month, a woman sat on a wobbly stool next to me. We talked about the wobbly stool and discovered that we were both authors and that she'd been reading my books for many years. I asked her about her book and we went to the local bookstore together, where I bought her book and she autographed it.

⊚ BeiNG delighTed By and AppreciATive of THe MirAcles.
WHile compleTiNG THe HandwriTiNG For This BOOK,
I weNT To THe BEACH and Asked to MEET A
MirAculous person. I SAW A MAN WEAriNG BrigHTly
Colored tenNis sHoes, drawiNG entrancinG syMBols
in THe sand. of course I stopped To TALK WiTH
HiM and found ovT THAT He WAS A Former GrAffiTi
ArTist, NOW A FAMOUS visioNNry ARTist WHo trAvels
THe worlD pAintiNG visioNAry MurALs. I drew MY NAME
iN THe sand and His eyes liT up: "YoU KNOW SNRK?"
I told Him THAT I WAS SNRK, and He exclAiMed:
"Yov meAn, SNRK SNRK-THE SNRK?" I love your work!
His NAME is XAVi, and we've decided To Be Friends.

WHile I WAS iN SaN Lvis OBispo CALiforNiA receNtly,
I WAS WALKiNG Aroved WiTH A WAd of Gum, lookiNG for A
plAce to THrow it AWAy. I turNed A corner and fouNd
A MirAcvlovs WALL of it!

Be A Transformational Change Agent

As we do our transformational work and learn to tell and live our new stories, we can assist others along the way to do the same.

I was at the Department of Motor Vehicles after buying a new car, and walked in to discover a lot of unhappy looking people and not so good energy. Everyone was clutching their papers and not speaking to each other. A strong feeling came over me, and I felt moved to stand up and sing

Amazing Grace

I sang the whole first verse by myself and then, behind me a woman joined in, then a man. By the third verse, most were singing, and the rest were smiling. By the last verse, the whole room had joined in, including the people working behind the bulletproof glass. When I had my turn with my papers, the agent thanked me for "changing the energy." We all changed the energy. And this could happen anywhere—not just in California.

On my next visit to the DMV, I heard a woman lamenting having bought a new car and not having her vehicle identification number, and needing to get back to work.

I advised her that the car dealership could fax it over, and the agent agreed. The woman seemed glad, and then joined me on the folding metal chairs and said with resignation:

"This is just my luck."

I felt amazed by her statement and asked her why. She said that she needed to get to work, that these things always happen to her, that everything is always difficult. I waited until she was done and replied:

"Wow—at least 3 people have helped you—me, the agent, and a person at the car dealership—and you're sitting here complaining and saying it's just your luck? How dare you!"

She just stared at me and finally said:

"WHO are you?"

I told her that I was a transformational change agent and so was she. That we can all learn to change our habituated negative stories, and help others to do the same.

I asked her if she'd be willing to tell the story differently — about 3 people helping her and not about things being "just her luck." She said she would.

I went back to this same office several months later to pick up a permit, and saw a woman clutching a paper in tears. I asked her what was wrong, and she said:

"I got a $275 ticket for being in a bus zone, and I wasn't even out of my car! I don't have the money to pay it, and my car is at a meter and it's going to run out of time before I can even see an agent!"

I said to her:

"Well, let's transform the situation!"
She asked how.

I told her I'd go put money in her meter, and she replied:

"It's 10 blocks away!"
I explained that I love walking. She said, "I don't have any quarters." I told her that I did. She finally blurted out:

"Why would you do this?"
I told her I was going to do it on one condition, and she asked what it was.

201

"THAT you BE A Transformational Change Agent and tell THIS STORY, and NOT THE one about THE $275 ticket and THE BUS zone— Agree?"

She Agreed. When I went to Her CAR 10 BlockS AWAY and pvt 8 quarters in Her Meter, I left Her A reminder note:

remember THAT you're A Transformational Change Agent- tell THose STories!

So I Know THAT putting THis Message in THis BOOK will spread THE MessAge More swiftly THan continuing To GO BACK To THe PMV, or telling People one By one.

and if course I'll Keep shNing with people one By one too!

I'M ASKing you To CHoose To Be A Transformational Change Agent and CHange your own BeHAviors and Stories, and when Appropriate, sHNe THAT Message with others.

"I fairly sizzle with zeal and enthusiasm, and spring forth with a mighty faith to do the things that ought to be done by me today."
Charles Fillmore

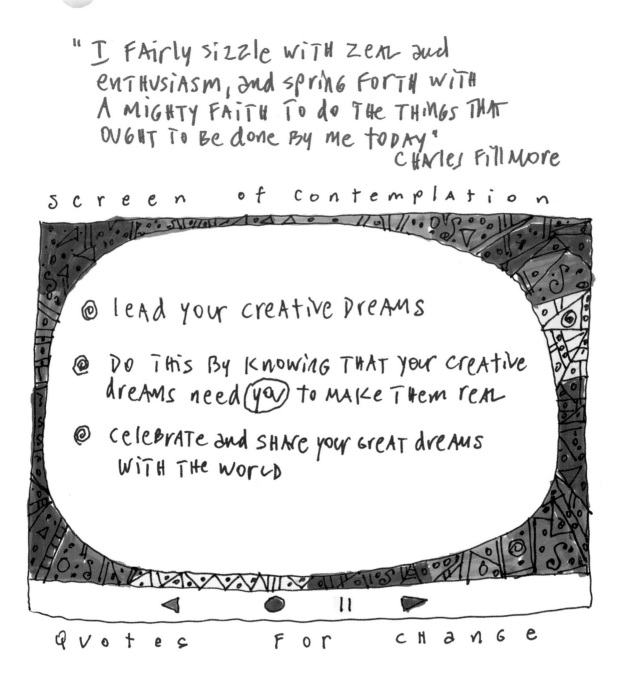

screen   of   contemplation

@ lead your creative dreams

@ do this by knowing that your creative dreams need (you) to make them real

@ celebrate and share your great dreams with the world

Quotes   for   change

"Joy is the most infallible sign of the presence of God"
Teilhard de Chardin

Transformation
Practices

•———

BOOKS

@ The spiritual dimension of The enneAGRAM
    SAudrA MAitri

@ eMBrAcing your inner Critic HALstone PH.D
                                sidrA stone PH.D
@ excuses BeGone WAyne Dyer

@ The inner Child WorKbook CATHRYN L. TAYler, M.A, M.F.C.C

@ Write stArts HAL ZinA Bennett

@ SARK's now CreAtive CompAnion SARK

@ The Promise of energy Psychology DAvid Feinstein PH.D
    DonnA eden, GUy CrAig

@ The Generosity PlAn KAtHy LeMAy

Web resources

@ plAneTSARK.com
@ enneAGRAMiNstitute.com
@ Delos-inc.com
@ MARYDisHAroon.com
@ OprAH.com
@ Ted.com
@ innersource.net
@ seAnecorn.com
@ arnortHrup.com

♪ MUSiC

MeditAtions for
eMotionAl HeAling
TArA BrACH PH.D

"THere Are THree sides To every story:
My side, your side, and THe TruTH.
And no one is Lying. memories
SHAred serve eAch one Differently"
robert evAns

Portraits
of
Joy and Transformation
Through change and loss

Introduction to the Glad portraits

For this book, I spoke with hundreds of people about transforming through change and loss.

I asked 8 questions, which are:

1. Describe a recent or longer-ago loss or change that has occurred in your life

2. What were/are your emotional/physical/spiritual responses? Describe in some detail all or one of them

3. What support did you receive? And if you didn't get the support you needed, why not?

4. How have you handled this loss or change, or others, badly or imperfectly?

5. What encouragement or advice can you offer to others experiencing loss and change? What works well for you?

6. How will/might you handle change or loss differently in the future as a result of your experiences?

7. What are the difficult aspects of loss or change for you?

8. Have you experienced any gifts in the midst of loss or change? List or describe them

Read the excerpts of the glad portraits on the following pages and be inspired by how change and loss affect us and give us opportunities for transformation.

Go to planetsark.com and read the rest of these glad portraits. And the rest we couldn't fit!

I've added a special section there with these glad portraits in their entirety, as well as a place where you can publish and share your own story.

I invite you to take my 8 questions and answer them, or change them, and add questions that encourage you further.

As we write and speak of transforming through change and loss, more gifts and opportunities will be revealed, and we see that we are not alone, and never were.

Shelly Mecum

Shelly is an inspirational author, speaker, mother, and middle school teacher. Her award-winning bestsellers include *God's Photo Album* and *The Watercolor Cat*. She lives in Honolulu, Hawaii.

Peggy Chun, renowned watercolor artist and my best friend, died November 19th, 2008, of ALS. Before she died, Peggy taught me how to live a life of joy and gratitude — especially in the face of grave adversity and loss.

I had years with Peggy to brace myself for her death. Peggy announced her decision to go off the ventilator and gave us all weeks to say goodbye and to tell her how many ways we loved her.

The children at my school helped me say goodbye to Peggy. They, too, loved her. Days before her death, the middle schoolers crowded into her bedroom and sang for her ("You Raise Me Up" by Josh Groban, "All You Need Is Love" by the Beatles, and Green Day's "Time of Your Life"), recited poetry, and read essays sharing how Peggy had changed their lives.

At school the next day, the children had a surprise for me. They had written letters of love and support and hidden them all over the classroom. I was finding letters for weeks afterward. And as the children and I sat and read aloud from *The Little Prince*, they didn't blink an eye when I asked if I could please cry. They simply ran for the tissues and brought me a Diet Coke.

The greatest advice I can share is what Peggy taught me. Whenever she felt herself spiraling into fear or self-pity, she played "the gratitude game" and made a mental list of everything she was grateful for. She always began with her family and friends. My list always begins with breathing. "I can breathe. I had a friend named Peggy who could not breathe on her own." Gratitude brings me right into the present moment, where everything is easier. "Seize the second" was one of Peggy's mottos.

Also, pay attention to your thoughts. Be sure they are words that soothe, strengthen, and encourage. Every thought should be steeped in tenderness and love. I like to talk to myself as if I were a five-year-old. It is quite soothing.

Self-love is critical. I consciously made myself a project — Project Shelly. I focused on my needs, on ways of cheering myself up. Would a little shopping help? A bubble bath? A run? Some hot soup? I accepted and acknowledged all the dark waves of emotion. I would simply say to myself, "Oh, you are sad right now. Who wouldn't be?" And I cried and cried.

I grow stronger with each loss and change. I grow braver, more deliberate. I choose the hero's path. If you pretend to be a superhero, you end up becoming one.

In the midst of my loss I have learned to value suffering. Through suffering, my soul grows and becomes "a force of goodness" (— Susan Arnout Smith). No matter how helpless or despairing I may feel, I can choose to shine joy. And when it's the darkest, I have learned to be still and watch for the miracles.

NATALIE ZEITUNY

Natalie is the founder of NZconsulting and the Conscious Business Center, a published author, a healer, and a teacher. www.nataliezeituny.com

When I was five years old, my little world shattered abruptly. *There is a war in Beirut*, they told me, and *we are the enemy*. As Jews in Lebanon, we were under serious threat. I saw buildings crumbling down, ruins piling up, fires, explosions, men with guns shouting. My 18-year-old brother was injured and died shortly after. My family had to run away, leaving behind everything we had. Israel welcomed us. I remember what it felt like — anxiety filtering into my blood and under my skin with every breath I took.

I've experienced many other losses since, but my early childhood loss was the most significant, since it penetrated a cellular level of my being and created deep anxiety and a feeling of insecurity in the world. Now, as I am transitioning out of the anxiety and mistrust, I feel a profound restfulness and peace, as if I am resting on Mount Everest.

How will I handle change or loss differently in the future as a result of my experiences? I will share about my loss, I will write poetry to my loss, I will dance to my loss. I will talk to my grief, be gentle with her, nurture her and love her unconditionally, no matter how messy, weak, and shaky she is. I will talk to her and create little rituals for her, for little Natalie who lost her brother, little Natalie who had to run away from Lebanon, little Natalie who survived a war, little Natalie who lost deep love. All these parts of me deserve a ritual, a ceremony, tears, and chocolate.

The most difficult aspect of loss is feeling as if I am standing naked on a cold winter day and everyone is watching. I am looking for a place to hide. That feeling of nakedness, of the vulnerability of the gentle human body and soul, is the biggest challenge for me.

My losses have given me the gift of a strong knowing that even the worst loss passes like a cloud; that I am stronger than iron; that I have created, orchestrated, and attracted all the losses in my life in order to grow and learn; that it is okay for my heart to experience pain; that it is human to give permission to my heart and soul to experience pain; that very soon my body-mind and spirit are always taken into a whole new realm of experiences. Learning to receive, to be humble, and to be vulnerable is the biggest gift of all.

MARNEY MAKRIDAKIS

Marney is the founder of Artella Land, a pioneering online playground and support community for writers, artists, and creative entrepreneurs.   www.artellaland.com

When I had my first child, I was 37, had a very full life, and did not understand how radically his arrival would change things. Of course I knew *intellectually* that my life would change, but I had no idea what that really meant: not just a "change" but a *complete* reinvention. I had no idea I would experience a paradoxical combination of deep loss and tremendous gain.

I had a complicated pregnancy and delivery, and as a result of the physical stress, I got Bell's palsy right after my son was born, which left one side of my face completely paralyzed. Happily, this condition was completely reversed within a few months, but emotionally and spiritually I continued to feel completely *asymmetrical*. On the one hand, I had this beautiful baby and I loved him deeply and marveled at the experience of caring for him. On the other hand, I felt like I had lost my sense of who I was, where I was, and the earth beneath me. I wasn't able to open my heart to my baby in the way I wanted to, and that was very surprising to me.

In hindsight, I realize I didn't take advantage of the support I could have had. For one thing, I felt ashamed, embarrassed, and sad about my feelings, so I was reluctant to share them with anyone. I thought it best to ignore and/or deal with the feelings in my own awkward, limited ways rather than truly expressing myself and reaching out to get support. Also, I was convinced that between caring for a newborn, dealing with my health issues, and keeping my business alive during the changing economy, there wasn't time for anything else. I didn't have the perspective to realize that reaching out and receiving support would end up giving me more time in the end.

The most dramatic element of this change was how unexpected it was. I'd like to think that as a result I'm becoming more adept at *anticipating* changes, and having better foresight about how various life changes might affect me and others.

My greatest challenges with any loss lie in just *being* with the feelings. To sit and really *feel* it is so much harder than escaping via the variety of methods I've used at various points in my life to emotionally flee.

My son is now two years old, and the gifts of parenthood *faaaaar* outweigh the losses! Now that I have settled into motherhood, and am continuing to navigate the curious shifts of personal identity, I am experiencing more joy and fullness in other roles: wife, friend, and business owner.

When I look back at any loss or change in my life — even the most painful ones — I can always, without exception, see the gift. It is *always* there, waiting to be revealed, and that is the gift of the life cycle.

TRISHA MARCY

Trisha lives in Eugene, Oregon, with her husband, aka Shmoopie, and their dog daughter, Molly. She owns her own virtual assistance practice and is known as Top Notch Trisha (TNT) by her dream client, SARK.

At age 22, I married the man who had been my boyfriend since the summer we met at age 16. We were divorced seven months later when he admitted he was gay.

It was one of the hardest things I've ever dealt with. My emotional response and state were up and down and all over the place. It wasn't just the end of my marriage (which is, of course, a big deal); I was also questioning myself as a woman: *Did I do something to cause this? Am I not attractive? How could he be gay and tell me he loved me for the past seven years?*

Also, we decided not to share this secret with anyone for a while, so I was alone in my suffering. I had just started a new job and shared my wedding news, photos, and joy with everyone there. I wished I could quit my job and run away to somewhere new where no one knew me, where no one knew this secret — because everyone wants to know why a marriage only lasts seven months. Then I found books on the subject (specifically, *The Other Side of the Closet* by Amity Buxton), and I didn't feel so alone.

The advice I would give to others going through loss is this: you are not alone. This helps me every time. There are books, support groups, message boards — other human beings who have experienced and are experiencing the same loss you are. Knowing that I'm not the only one helps me to not question God/the Universe/Higher Beings with the quintessential "Why me?" (I've found the answer to this to be "Why not me?")

The most difficult aspects of loss are that it seems to happen at the worst times and that I have absolutely zero control over it. Letting go and trusting is difficult. I keep practicing anyway, and I am getting better at it.

Through this loss, I found support and love and friendship in unexpected places. My heart was opened when I marched in gay pride parades with PFLAG (Parents, Families and Friends of Lesbians and Gays) and saw parents who completely love and support their gay children. This experience has allowed me to welcome all kinds of human beings into my life, to not judge or hate anyone because of who they love.

I've learned about myself — searching and reaching and growing. Going to counseling, reading books, wanting to be a better person. Wanting to not give up on love and a joyful life because sometimes "bad" things happen.

And after my divorce, I found a man who has completely and totally loved me for the past 14 years. Who didn't mind being asked "Are you gay?" for the first few years. A man who keeps his heart open when mine starts closing over worry and fear. I know love again.

Leslie Lewis Sword

Leslie is an actress and author whose most well-known work is the solo show Miracle in Rwanda, the inspiring story of genocide survivor Immaculée Ilibagiza.   www.miracleinrwanda.com

When I was a sophomore in college, my father died after a short illness, leaving behind my mom, my sister, and me. For a year before his death, I had had premonitions about it, even though he was only 49 and healthy. When he actually died, I realized there must be more to this world than meets the eye, because there was no rational way for me to have known that he would die. It opened my eyes to the possibility of the world of Spirit.

I have since learned that there is a gift in every experience, and if I immediately turn my attention to what the situation makes me want for myself, I feel better. I look for the hidden gift. So, in this case, the hidden gift was learning that really, there is no death. The energy of my father still exists, in my mind's eye, and when I'm feeling good, I can connect with him. The consolation of that connection sustains me.

I try to see the benefit of every situation now. My father's death became a wonderful experience in so many ways. It made me into a lifelong seeker. What is difficult about that is — I now know that I create my own life, so there are no excuses.

I now know that death is not the end, but while we are here, we are meant to live joyful lives. I do my best to live joyfully, and when I'm not, I try to take exquisite care of myself. I wrote a poem about it!

JOY

I'm so happy!
I'm the happiest I've ever been!
And I know how to do it now.

If I am thinking of you
and you are far from me
I send you a postcard
from my heart
And then you are with me.

But also

I have ME now.

I will always have me
I will never leave me
I will always love me

VALERIE TATE

Val is a marriage and family therapist in private practice working with adults, couples, kids, families, and groups. She lives in San Francisco.   www.valtate.com

I went from hero to black sheep overnight when I came out to my family as being bisexual and in love with a woman. I had always been very close to my family and couldn't imagine anything that could divide us or make me want to spend less time with them. Also, I had always been very accepted in my life. As the "hero" child, I had felt powerful and celebrated.

When I came out, their response was shocking. I lost my father's respect because he didn't agree with the choice I had made. I lost my mother's faith in my values and morals. My brother became a preacher and turned away from me, and my sister couldn't relate to me because I was now "different" from her as a woman. I had never before realized the difference between love and acceptance. Now I knew they loved me, but I had lost their acceptance.

For two years I had to call my parents several times to hear back from them (we all used to talk daily). I went from confidence to nervousness speaking to my father, as if I were waiting for him to approve of me again. I felt desperate for a morsel of my old relating with him. My mother quoted the Bible in every conversation. Each family member I spoke to tried to convince me to feel and act differently.

Before the rupture I didn't realize how much I had measured my growth professionally and personally through the lens of my family. Being the black sheep was extremely uncomfortable. Hearing my inner voice was so difficult when I allowed my need for approval to enter the scene.

It was a huge loss of identity to not feel close to my family, especially my parents. They thought I had changed into another person, so I felt unseen and misunderstood. I was the same little me inside, yet I felt like an orphan.

I was impatient with my family for not adjusting to my changes. I judged them for being judgmental. I had always prided myself on accepting others, even if they were different. I was the person in the family whom others turned to with their secrets and isolation when they felt unaccepted. So after all the years I had accepted them for who they were, I felt owed the same service.

I supported myself by meditating often to remove negative energy or thoughts about who I am and how I live my life and truth. I also talked to close friends about it when it came up.

My advice to others going through loss or change is this: Accept what is. When change happens, it nearly always puts your identity in question. Generously and gently ask yourself who you are now, today. Learn to love and accept yourself and your process in the change, and let others grow at their own pace.

Brian andreas

Brian is the artist & writer behind Story People. He is known worldwide for his lyrical stories & colorful artwork rendered in prints, books & found wood sculptures. He lives in Santa Barbara, California.   www.storypeople.com

Where can I begin? It's probably best to start a couple of years ago. My wife of 28 years, Ellen, had late stage III breast cancer, followed by 14 rounds of chemo & a bilateral mastectomy. After that, our elder son developed testicular cancer & went through the intensity of the chemo that particular cancer demands. Our younger son developed some weird stomach & gall bladder thing that we've yet to understand. He lives in a world of constant nausea & frequent vomiting. These events, along with the hum of endless medical tests, seemed to be the music of our lives.

Oh, one more thing. Before all these events threw their fireworks across our skies, I had started work on a project that excited me like nothing else had for a long, long time. I felt like everything I had ever done in my life — my art, my writing, my strange side roads — all had led me up to this point. That I was being given an invitation. It was an invitation that had me say yes, with all my heart.

One morning, I woke up & told Ellen I was leaving. I told her I loved her & the boys but had no more husbanding left in me. I've always had a pretty good tool kit for dealing with the weirdness of the world (probably the result of a childhood with two psychologists as parents), but I found I suddenly had no map whatsoever. It felt like the only way to survive was to leave.

I don't know if it will ever make sense. From the outside, it looked like I left a good marriage & a beautiful family at their time of greatest need, to go work on an exciting new project. From the inside, it felt inevitable & mythic, a riddle from the Sphinx with neither clear questions nor clear answers.

My wife has been cancer-free now for almost two years & has recovered her vibrancy & health fully. She's begun to sing again, creating a world of music & beauty around her. My elder son is cancer-free & regaining his strength steadily. There are days he still feels like an 80-year-old, with his joints creaking & his energy ebbing & flowing, but he sees recovery coming closer. My younger son feels better each week, still with nausea, but no longer so baffled by the arbitrary nature of its appearances. My family is moving toward their own new relationship with the world.

& me? I'm still excited by the work I'm doing. Still not quite sure what happened, or why, but trusting that it is a pathway I need to follow. There is much that's unresolved, but now I'm more able to simply sit with that. To know that I will understand when I understand. Until then, I'm just glad to be here, experiencing it all....

The writer of this piece is a freelance editor living in the San Francisco Bay Area.

As I write this, my bankruptcy will be final in less than two weeks. On that day, the creditors will have no more claim on me, and my debts will be cleared.

I've been in debt my whole adult life. Because I was conscientious about paying on time, I had a good credit rating and was able to borrow more and more. Eventually, I was borrowing on one account to pay another. As the debt mounted, I indulged in magical thinking: I'd land another well-paying job (which sometimes did happen); I'd come up with a moneymaking business; some deus ex machina would bring in more money (this also happened a couple of times). But the influxes of money never lasted long, and over the last couple of years, the recession hit my business. Finally I took a good look at my debt and realized that even if I somehow were able to make the minimum payments, I might be paying out over a thousand dollars a month for the rest of my life and never be able to save for retirement.

The decision to file for bankruptcy felt shocking, as though I'd been launched into a different reality. It went against my self-image of always being "responsible." The shame and disorientation of going into bankruptcy, combined with the extensive accounting necessary for the application, felt like walking through fire.

As soon as I decided to file, I stopped using credit. It was helpful not to have to pay out all that money every month, but I'm self-employed, and for the first time in my adult life I was spending only what I actually had in the bank, which fluctuates from month to month. Suddenly my earnings — the fruits of my labor — became real in a way that they had never been before.

For the first time, I began to do something I'd never had the patience for before: shopping for bargains, being careful about how I spent my money. It feels good to spend 30 to 50 percent less on a grocery bill, and to see my money stay in my checking account longer. Now I see the direct relationship between my work and the goods and services I buy, and therefore I value the effort and time of my work much more. I feel more fully alive, because I think the denial I was in — the denial that allowed me to always be in debt — necessitated a kind of moral drowsiness. So my bankruptcy — one of society's main symbols of loss — has been a transformational experience for which I am grateful.

TAMA KiEVES

Tama is the founder of Awakening Artistry and the bestselling author of *This Time I Dance!: Creating the Work You Love.*   www.AwakeningArtistry.com

I left my job as an attorney in an elite law firm and lost my career, security, and identity in the process. Even though I quit the job, the decision felt choiceless. I couldn't exist another day there.

I'd always been "the golden girl." I'd graduated with honors from Harvard Law School and risen to partnership track. I'd always chased other people's approval and external success. Leaving a familiar world meant all the rules changed on me. I lost my friends and colleagues, my income, a handy description of my employment, and my context. It was terrifying, and somehow more unsettling because I had "chosen" it.

This loss pulled up a great deal of my childhood pain. While I was growing up, "the real me" — sensitive, creative, and free-spirited — was never seen and appreciated. So I buried the real me and became "the successful me," the one family and teachers praised. When I left law, I had to deal with the original pain, the root ache of not having been seen or valued for my true self. I had to learn to feel my feelings. Physically, I was exhausted. The overwhelming sense of freedom and responsibility to figure out the next part of my life was terrifying, and the weight of it crushed me.

The most radical support for me was discovering that I had a Beloved Inner Voice. I began studying the spiritual psychotherapy program A Course in Miracles and then teaching it. I found out just how loved I am in this lifetime. I discovered I have a way to get through anything — until the next loss, that is, when, no doubt, I will forget most of this and have to relearn it.

Here's what I like to tell my coaching clients going through loss or change: The tremendous energy of pain, defeat, or resistance you feel will transmute and heal into love, creativity, and strength. A loss shapes you and creates you, like negative space in a painting. Carl Jung said, "Where you are wounded, you are gifted." Every loss in my life has demanded that I incorporate it into my identity and birth a new realization, capacity, or calling because of it.

I also believe it helps, so much, just to feel your feelings. Honor yourself by telling your story and listening to the story with mercy, dignity, and interest. Your inner voice and creativity will offer you miraculous clues for your healing.

One of the amazing gifts I have gotten out of all this: I trust and value my creativity. It is no longer something I try to hold back so that I can function in a "normal" life — that is, stay true to what is not me. My creativity is my greatest resource of freedom and power, a form of genius that gives every aspect of this life meaning and provides me with an inspired approach to everything.

McNair Wilson

McNair is an actor, director, teacher, playwright, former Disney Imagineer, public-speaking and creativity coach, cartoonist, magician, and ventriloquist (retired). Also an author, he offers keynote presentations and workshops on creative thinking and inventive problem solving. www.mcnairwilson.com

In 1992, I experienced the deaths of my favorite uncle in February, my father in April, and my mother in July. Having been quite close to both of my parents and my Uncle Paul, I always knew that when they each died the loss would be deep and strongly felt, but that before long I would be able to celebrate our long years together. And so I did. My Christian faith assures me that we will be together again, and that is a grand and reassuring sense in my life. But I still miss them constantly. My faith fills me with hope to carry on with my life. I cannot imagine how I would have experienced their deaths and lived with their absence if God were not in my life.

In the case of my parents, both my brother and I believe that the quality of the lives we lead is a lasting tribute to our great parents. Whenever I feel like my unorthodox way of navigating life seems to rub people or institutions the wrong way, I am buoyed by the fact that my folks both supported my individuality — including when I attended a private school where my dad was principal. I was sent to his office for discipline frequently.

It is so important to do all we can to build powerful bonds with those closest to us while we are still together. Even the very best relationships take work, every day. Do the work. It's worth it. When we do this, I have learned, our loved ones' passing is harder to live through at the time of their death but our lives remain rich with their presence — so much of them continues to dwell in our hearts and spirits on a daily basis.

It is difficult to deal with the randomness of some who die "too young" or in the prime of their creative contribution to life. Meanwhile, others live long lives and never seem to find their passion or hit their stride. It is all part of the grand mystery of life that frustrates and confuses. But I would have it no other way, for without the mystery there would be no flavor, no color, none of the many unexpected joys as we discover life unfolding, improvisationally, each day.

If we notice the flavors and colors of life as we live it, they become the powerful and lasting memories that we carry with us long after the loss of friends and close family members. I catch glimpses of those I lost in 1992 — in the way a stranger tilts their head like my mother did, smirks like my dad, or holds a paintbrush and makes a knowing stroke like Uncle Paul. If we notice, they live on and so do we.

andrea scher

Andrea is a creative entrepreneur, writer, and life coach living in Berkeley, California.
www.superherodesigns.com/journal   www.MondoBeyondo.org

A collection of important friendships in my life fell away at the same time. My response to these friendship "breakups" was to go into a really dark place for about a year. I bumped up against my darkest stuff there, wondering what was wrong with me, if I was broken beyond repair, if the ways in which I was imperfect were simply too unsavory for the world. It touched into my most basic and primal fears about worth: *Was I worthy of being alive? Was I worthy of being loved?*

I received the greatest comfort and most loving support from a few dear friends in my life. My oldest friends, especially from childhood, continued to reflect back to me my goodness and what they knew was true about me (beyond whatever fears I had). They somehow affirmed who I was at my core, who I have always been, and I took refuge in their truth. They were my anchor.

The loss that I experienced — like most losses, I suppose — came out of left field. I didn't choose it, and if I could have prevented it, I would have. Nevertheless, it is always *what we do with what life hands us* that matters most.

I believe that my spirit was ready for healing and growth, and my responsibility was simply to show up for that. Sometimes the breakdown is the breakthrough.

My advice to others is to trust what life hands us, to create something out of the messes we are given, to *use* every experience to learn how to love ourselves and others better.

The difficult aspects of loss and change, besides the obvious discomforts, are that they ask us to change right alongside them. They ask us to be more courageous, have deeper compassion, and trust ourselves more. They ask us to stretch and grow in big ways, and they don't ask permission first.

Loss and change also ask us an important question: *How will we respond?* They ask us to put to use all the spiritual tools we have collected. It's where the rubber meets the road and where our Jedi training gets put into practice.

I believe that gifts come with every significant experience in our lives and with loss and change, in particular. As we deepen our capacity for grief, compassion, and even sorrow, we carve out space for more joy. Our range increases, and we are able to hold more than before. Our hearts are tenderized from life's battles, and we become more supple and open. We also become a safer place for others to land, a kind of sanctuary.

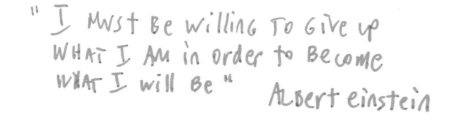

"I must be willing to give up
what I am in order to become
what I will be"   Albert einstein

screen   of   contemplation

@ create willingness

@ Do this by exploring Areas of resistance,
releasing them, and welcoming Acceptance

@ Accelerate your willingness practices
by being in a consistent state of
inspiration

◀   ●   ❚❚   ▶

Quotes   For   change

"You must think that something is
happening with you, that life has not
forgotten you, that it holds you in its
Hand and will not let you fall"
                        rilke

Portraits
of
Joy and Transformation
Through change and loss

"Easy is right. Begin easy
and you are easy, continue
easy and you are right.
The right way to go easy
is to forget the right way
and forget that the going
is easy"
CHUANG TZU

BOOKS

- Intimacy and Solitude Stephanie Dowrick
- The invitation Oriah
- Imagine a Woman in love with herself Patricia Lynn reilly
- Women, food and God Geneen roth
- The Book of Qualities ruth Gendler
- Positive energy Judith orloff

web resources

- Oriahmountaindreamer.com
- imagineawoman.com
- cosmiccowgirlsmakemillionaires.com
- cuteoverload.com
- Kripalu.org
- Forgivenessalliance.org
- garyrosenthal.net

"Your body is the lifeforce power of
some fifty million molecular geniuses.
You and you alone choose moment by
moment who and how you want to be
in the world"
Jill Bolte Taylor

SARK SAYS YES TO NEW WORLD LIBRARY! WHAT A GOOD COMPANY

NEW WORLD LIBRARY is dedicated to publishing books and other media that inspire and challenge us to improve the quality of our lives and the world.

We are a socially and environmentally aware company, and we strive to embody the ideals presented in our publications. We recognize that we have an ethical responsibility to our customers, our staff members, and our planet.

We serve our customers by creating the finest publications possible on personal growth, creativity, spirituality, wellness, and other areas of emerging importance. We serve New World Library employees with generous benefits, significant profit sharing, and constant encouragement to pursue their most expansive dreams.

As a member of the Green Press Initiative, we print an increasing number of books with soy-based ink on 100 percent postconsumer-waste recycled paper. Also, we power our offices with solar energy and contribute to nonprofit organizations working to make the world a better place for us all.

Our products are available
in bookstores everywhere.
For our catalog, please contact:

New World Library
14 Pamaron Way
Novato, California 94949

Phone: 415-884-2100 or 800-972-6657
Catalog requests: Ext. 50
Orders: Ext. 52
Fax: 415-884-2199
Email: escort@newworldlibrary.com

To subscribe to our electronic newsletter, visit
www.newworldlibrary.com

ACKnowledguents and Appreciations To:

Every reader and Participant in The realm of SARK. I Heartily Thank you. All The professionals who wisely escort me: TRISHA MARCY "T.N.T." Top Notch Trisha and The whole team at planet SARK. everyone at IWB, steve Musick and everyone at Destiny Capital. Debra Goldstein, Mary Ann Naples and every Library and Bookstore.

And To My Beautifull Tribe of Friends and Family

My vision for us All

We each become and live like "full cups of self-love" sharing the overflow, and not half empty cups trying to get filled.

We consistently do our transformative work and become "Transformational change agents" taking action in the world.

We pause to admire the moon

We feel our feelings and practice finding the glad parts in all of them.

We embody the spirit of "Glad No Matter What" and transform our losses into gifts and our changes into opportunities—All of our lives.

love, Susan (AKA SARK)

San Francisco California Aug 8 2010

A Transformational Change Sheet

Give yourself the gift of change. Fill out this sheet, ask a friend or loved one to mentor you in your process of transformation

I choose to transform: _____

_____

I can't, won't, haven't yet because: _____

_____

I positively challenge myself to: _____

_____

I am resisting my positive challenge because: _____

_____

I am willing to change: _____

_____

I am glad about: _____

_____

_____